The Schools
we have

THE
SCHOOLS
WE WANT

James Nehring

The Schools we have

THE SCHOOLS WE WANT

An American
Teacher
on the
Front Line

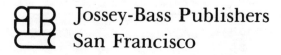 Jossey-Bass Publishers
San Francisco

For sales outside the United States, contact Maxwell Macmillan International Publishing Group, 866 Third Avenue, New York, New York 10022.

Manufactured in the United States of America

The paper used in this book is acid-free and meets the State of California requirements for recycled paper (50 percent recycled waste, including 10 percent postconsumer waste), which are the strictest guidelines for recycled paper currently in use in the United States.

Library of Congress Cataloging-in-Publication Data

Nehring, James.
    The schools we have, the schools we want : an American teacher on the front line / James Nehring. — 1st ed.
      p.   cm. — (The Jossey-Bass education series)
    Includes bibliographical references.
    ISBN 1-55542-457-0 (alk. paper)
    1. High school teaching—United States.   2. High school students—United States.   I. Title II. Series.
LB1737.U6N43   1992
373.11′02′0973—dc20   92-14016
                                               CIP

FIRST EDITION
HB Printing   10 9 8 7 6 5 4 3 2 1   *Code 9270*

The
Jossey-Bass
Education
Series

Contents

x   Contents

Preface

Five years ago I wrote *Why Do We Gotta Do This Stuff, Mr. Nehring?: Notes from a Teacher's Day in School*. Readers told me they liked the book because it was different from all the big reports that came out in the 1980s on The Crisis in Education. My book was "real world," they said. Now, all the talk is about school reform and the big reports have shifted their focus from the *crisis* in education to *solutions*. There are bold new visions and plans for restructured schools. But because I sense in the latest reports the same kind of unreal quality that prompted my readers' earlier comments, I decided it's time to write another book.

The field of school-reform literature is dominated by university researchers, think tank experts, journalists, "consultants," and public officials. Their insights are often valid, their advice often sound, and I readily acknowledge a debt to many whose work I've read (see my endnotes). But they *all* write as school outsiders. None works with kids on a regular basis. None starts every morning in a high school classroom and rides out the day with a hundred-plus students who are sometimes cooperative, sometimes not. And none has real access to that internal adult world of high school: the faculty meetings, the memos, the parent conferences, the talk around the copy machine.

Let me take you, then, inside Amesley Junior-Senior High School, the setting of *Why Do We Gotta Do This Stuff, Mr. Nehring?*, and there let us see what happens when tidy theories of reform and restructuring meet up with the very messy human reality of school. There's a brand-new principal. Her name is Roberta Walters, and she's finding out very quickly about the gulf between theory and practice. Then there's Mr. Nehring and some of his colleagues. You know the type: head-in-the-clouds dreamers who think they can change the system. There are also some tough-minded veteran teachers who've seen it all. And there are parents and board members, administrators and kids. Join us all as we ride the crest of the school-reform wave over a period of two years. Will real change come to Amesley High?

This is a story, not a report. It does not announce a thesis and marshal supporting evidence. It tells a tale. It has characters and plot, drama and humor, and maybe a little bit of mischief. It does not suggest any particular instructional strategy or organizational theory, but it gestures toward certain truths about teaching, learning, and institutional change. If you've read the reports on school reform, all of which offer an important outside perspective, please now read this, a view from the inside.

Finally, this is a work of fiction. Though it draws heavily on my own experience and is intended to be realistic, it is *not* real. With respect to characters especially, I strongly discourage anyone from drawing parallels to people I have worked with. The characters in this book are not simply "masked," they are completely made up. Indeed, in some cases where characters strayed too close to real people I know, I made alterations in the final manuscript.

Many have given generously of their talent and their time to assist me in the project that ultimately became this book. In particular I would like to thank several fellow writers who endured long group sessions of reading (and rereading): Pauline Bartel, Jackie Craven, Dave Drotar, Joyce Hunt, Kate Kunz, Maureen Lewicki, Peg Lewis, Marie Musgrove, Jane Streiff, and Donna Tomb; also, Ann Connolly, Terri Goldrich, Richard Hughes, Jocelyn Jerry, Peggy O'Rourke, Robin Rapaport, Asta Roberts, and James Yeara. Thanks also go to two colleagues who read the completed manuscript, Dominick DeCecco and Jon Hunter. Thanks also to Lesley Iura, who championed the manuscript at Jossey-Bass. I am grateful, especially, to members of my extended family who cheerfully welcome me on holiday visits even though they know I always arrive with a manuscript.

July 1992 James Nehring
Delmar, New York

For Laurie and Rebecca,
with all my love.

The Author

James Nehring teaches social studies and English at Bethlehem Central High School in Delmar, New York. He is the author of *Why Do We Gotta Do This Stuff, Mr. Nehring?: Notes from a Teacher's Day in School* (1989) and serves on the editorial board of *Social Science Record* as book review editor. His work has appeared in the *Washington Post, Education Week,* and *Social Science Record,* and he has made guest appearances on CNN and National Public Radio.

Nehring earned his B.A. degree with high distinction (1980) from the University of Virginia and his master of arts degree in teaching (M.A.T., 1982) from Brown University. He has also studied at the University of Salzburg, in Austria, and is a doctoral candidate in education theory and practice at The University at Albany, State University of New York.

He records the following as especially memorable events: sailing the Nile River from Aswan to Luxor in an old wooden boat, playing his trumpet one night at a West Berlin nightclub near the Wall (which did not tumble down), arguing with Mario Cuomo about the importance of class size, working as sous-chef for a French restaurant, proposing marriage to Laurie at the bottom of the Grand Canyon, making home-brewed beer with his father, talking backstage with Dizzy Gillespie, receiving an affirmative response at the Canyon rim, serving as faculty advisor to the always controversial student newspaper, singing "Edelweiss" with Rebecca, climbing Cathedral Ledge in New Hampshire, corresponding with Uncle Bix.

James Nehring lives with his wife, Laurie, and daughter, Rebecca. He is at work on a novel about best friends.

They always say that
time changes things,
but you actually have to
change them yourself.
Andy Warhol

1.

Who's Accountable Here Anyway?

". . . the square kind. You know, the kind that comes out one sheet at a time. Little square pieces. Hard and coarse. I mean, the stuff might as well be sandpaper."

As a late joiner to the school management team, I had to be caught up on important items already under discussion. I was a late joiner because Don Diegl, who had served for several months, decided one day that he was already overcommitted. He had too many papers to correct anyway since he was an English teacher and couldn't Roberta, the new principal, find someone else to volunteer to fill the spot? Don really did support the concept of shared decision making but he himself just couldn't see his way clear right now and maybe next year and he was very sorry. So Roberta asked me. Which is why on a Thursday afternoon in December I found myself in Conference Room A with four other teachers and the principal, getting caught up on old business.

"But Roberta should tell it," said English teacher Bill Pierce, who had been trying to fill me in but to whom I was

1

obviously showing signs of disbelief. So Bill deferred to Roberta Walters, captain of our ship.

"Yes, it really is true," Roberta began. "We've been talking about toilet paper—among other things—for, well, I guess a couple months now. I know it's crazy, but I figure if this is what the faculty wants to test me on, if we're going to play this game, then let's play it."

"They're testing you?" I asked. Roberta Walters was entering her fourth month as principal of Amesley High; she had replaced Ralph Peters, who'd moved to the greener pastures of Chester School District, where he was now superintendent.

"Yeah," said Roberta. "Okay . . ." Roberta was realizing she'd have to tell the long version. "Middle of September, a petition appears on my desk. It says, 'We, the undersigned, want normal toilet paper in the faculty bathrooms' or something like that. At first, I was kind of upset that they thought they had to resort to a petition to get my attention. But then I thought, okay, I'd see what I could do, figuring it should be easy enough. So, first I come to the school management team. I present the issue. There's a motion to vote. We vote. The idea gets approved. Democracy in action, right? Next I go to the head of maintenance. Al D'Abruzzi is a very capable guy and a very cooperative guy. Al says fine, take care of it in a day. His staff will put in new retainers so that rolled toilet paper may be installed and he'll order rolled toilet paper to install into the new retainers. Problem solved. I sent off a memo to my petitioners: 'To the undersigned, your petition is granted.'

"Only there are problems. Al comes back a week later and says the vendor that we buy toilet paper from sells in bulk to the entire district and if we're going to change the order, we have to change the whole order. So I call up the vendor, and he says Al's right. I explain the situation and suggest how about if after the order is delivered, I come back to the warehouse with so many boxes and trade them in for rolls of equal value. He hems and haws. Finally, he says okay.

"There's more. Three days go by. I get a memo—from the office of the assistant superintendent for business and finance, O. Braxton Sandersen. Dr. Sandersen informs me that I may not tamper with requisition orders originating in the central office as it interferes with accounting and please see that it does not happen again. So all of a sudden I'm an outlaw just because I want to change the goshdarn toilet paper. I mean, I start having these visions of stealing over to the vendor's warehouse at midnight with coal on my face, you know, and bribing the night watchman. It's crazy."

Welcome to Amesley Junior-Senior High School, a make-believe place that stands for much in American public education. Amesley is a kind of Everyschool, and the tale that is told here will sound disturbingly familiar to people everywhere who are involved in public education. Amesley (the town) is a middle-class suburb—more than half of all American kids live in suburbs—and this is a tale of what goes on behind the scenes of American education in the mainstream.[1] Though Amesley is itself fictionalized—the characters, events, and setting are all composites based on my own experience in several school systems—the issues embedded in this tale are very real indeed.

The time is 1990. The date is important, because it places us at the end of a long decade of so-called school reform. A decade that began with *A Nation at Risk,* that clarion call to action from a presidential commission, and witnessed a great parade of scholarly reports and proposals all announcing with trumpet and bass drum the errors of the system and the dawning of a new era in public education. As the marching bands went by, more and more schools, school districts, and sometimes whole states began to join in. There were plenty of new marching songs: restructuring, teacher empowerment, site-based management, back to basics, accountability, early intervention. The momentum was building. It promised to be an era of great change. Schools as we had known them since the Industrial Revolution would be somehow (nobody was quite sure how) swept away and replaced by futuristic institutions that would meet the needs of all kids, save society from its multiple ills, and, above all, keep us competitive with the Japanese.

It didn't happen. It turns out schools and the institutional norms that shape them are not easily manipulated. While all the big reports envisioned reformed schools, they said very little about the process of getting from where we now are to where they would have liked us to be. It turns out that schools are ultimately *human* institutions and as such do not always respond in entirely rational and predictable ways.

This book is about school as a human institution. It is about the quirky, often irrational manner in which the people who make up a school respond to the poking and prodding of reformism. But it is not merely a condemnation of human irrationality; it is also a celebration of certain nonrational qualities: passion, virtue. In sum, this is not a theoretical abstraction of human behavior, it is a reflection on the particular. This kind of reflection is not always pleasant, since that is the realm where foolishness dwells, but it is sometimes inspiring because it is also home to compassion and heroism.

Early in her tenure as principal of Amesley Junior-Senior High School, Roberta Walters was learning about inertia and the difficulty of change in public education, even modest change. Take the location of the monthly faculty meeting, for example. For years, faculty meetings were held in the Little Theatre, a kind of small auditorium with rows of cushy chairs descending to a small thrust stage. Here, Ralph Peters, erstwhile school principal, held forth for four and a half years. As he stepped to the stage from a side door, the lights would dim, the overhead projector would snap on, and on the screen would appear a transparency showing standardized test scores, or student averages, or student load. Ralph would say words like *median* and *mode* and *percentile* and *above average* and *outstanding results* and then the overhead would click off. Ralph would make announcements (with lights still dim) and then he would say he wanted our input on this or that or was there any feedback. And sometimes there would be no input or feedback and sometimes there would be a little but it was just a simple question to which Ralph would give a simple answer.

But more often the inputting and feedbacking developed into something like a dialogue, sometimes heated. Then Ralph would ask please for the lights to be turned up, which only fanned the flames because it got everybody's attention away from the tests they were correcting or averages they were calculating in those deep cushy chairs in the dim light, and they now had to look attentive. And just as they were becoming attentive, the feedbacking and inputting might be turning into a fight, with angry accusations falling like rotten tomatoes on the stage. Ralph would be holding forth and there would be much spleen venting and Ralph would suck it all in and try to look calm and dignified—and then suddenly it would be 3:30, which according to the teachers' contract is the time by which faculty meetings must end. So people would start to dribble out (union stalwarts first), and more would leave, and soon there'd be just a few hangers-on standing on the floor in front of that stage and Ralph would be standing at the edge of the stage addressing them. And the floor of the stage would be strewn with many rotten tomatoes.

This did not match the new principal's concept of the ideal faculty meeting. Roberta Walters determined that she would alter this long-standing ritual so as not to be the (sole) target of all those rotten tomatoes.

Roberta wanted to be a thoroughly modern high school principal, not the autocratic manipulator that so many of those school-reform reports had targeted as one of the problems of public education. No, she was going to establish collegial norms for policy-making at Amesley. One of her first acts was to establish the school management team, a representative group of teachers and other school personnel that would serve as her personal cabinet and offer the best advice as she attempted to transform our school. Furthermore, the school is a community, reasoned Roberta—a radical concept for Amesley High School—and we all must pull together to make this community work. The school principal cannot do it alone, it must be a group effort. And, since Ralph's kind of faculty meeting did not jibe with this concept of school as community, Roberta chose to inaugurate her principalship with a faculty meeting in the school cafeteria—the beginning, she hoped, of a new tradition.

So that's where we met. The lights did not dim; they stayed on, white and fluorescent. There was no stage, so Roberta just stood on the cafeteria floor. There were no cushy chairs in descending rows, so all the teachers just sat at those long rectangular cafeteria tables. Some of the teachers took advantage of this new situation to sit with their backs to that new principal since after all some of the chairs at those oblong tables were so oriented, and the teachers reasoned if this is what that new principal wants then this is what she gets. And some of the teachers sat right behind the big fat pillars that dotted the large cafeteria floor and figured here they could do their grades and correct essays. All in all it promised to be a different sort of a faculty meeting.

At that first meeting in the cafeteria, Roberta made some opening remarks about the school as a community and everybody working together and everyone responsible and how this new way of meeting as a faculty would reflect this collegial approach to education. And some teachers grumbled but most looked as if they were thinking, Well, okay we'll give it a shot. By and large teachers are good sports and even though most veteran Amesley teachers had seen a half dozen principals come and go over the years and even though they made jokes about the half life of a school administrator, this new principal was after all a person, probably a fairly well-intending person, and lord knows any job in the schools is hard so why not give her a break. She'll learn.

In general, good will characterized the meeting. There was talk about revamping the curriculum and taking a look at our scheduling practices and giving a look at our philosophy as a school. On their way out, faculty members were heard saying things like, "Well, for once it looks like instead of talking about smoking in the bathrooms and not enough parking spaces and kids late to class we'll be treating professional issues."

Hurray.

Sooner or later, the rhetoric of school reform must, however, meet up with the reality of the institution, a reality that includes that very uncollegial fact of life known as collective bargaining, a fact of life that so many of those big reports on school reform chose to ignore but that we at Amesley could not.

Roberta Walters's first year as principal coincided with the last year of the three-year negotiated agreement between the district and the teachers. Bargaining for a new contract had begun in October. In December, contract talks were declared to be at impasse, which meant that the teachers, with Jerry Rubicon as our chief negotiator, and the school district had been unable to make a deal. Now professional arbitrators would have to be brought in. A painful, potentially bitter, and probably long process would begin.

Morale plummeted. Principal and teachers were working in opposite directions. Roberta kept up a steady stream of school-as-community and let's-all-work-together, to which the teachers answered with community-my-ass and not-until-we-get-this-contract-signed. And more gripes started to surface about smokers in the bathrooms and kids late to class. Roberta was forming committees to investigate school philosophy and formulate goals and objectives and let's be bold and innovative and small groups and cooperative decision making and democratizing the workplace, and the teachers just said enough with committees, we're not volunteering!

December was a dark month. The union reps called a meeting. We met in the Little Theatre, which prompted a kind of psychic retrenchment. We had not assembled in the Little Theatre as a faculty since Ralph's last faculty meeting the previous June. At that meeting there had been no rotten tomatoes and there had even been applause for Ralph, who shed visible tears to a group of people he would leave behind for a superintendency at nearby Chester Central Schools. So there was this wave of nostalgia as the seats of the Little Theatre filled.

As the meeting began, it was clear from comments that

Roberta Walters's honeymoon period as new principal was over. It being a union meeting, Roberta of course was not there.

"If I hear about one more goddamned innovative idea, I think I'm gonna puke." This was Joe Grossi, who in September had been glad we were going to treat professional issues. Joe was stirred up. "We spend every faculty meeting talking about philosophy this and philosophy that and this committee and that committee. When are we gonna talk about the fact that this school is falling apart around us, that the kids are taking over the hallways, that the smokers in the bathroom laugh in my face, that the kids are parking their cars all over the lawn? You guys know what I mean."

Many comments like Joe's were made at this meeting. The meeting was supposed to be for us to discuss lack of progress with the contract, but it quickly became an exercise in spleen venting. Even people who rarely speak up spoke. Bernice Fleischmann said that what we really needed was male leadership because the kids just would not take a woman principal seriously. Generally, there was much administrator bashing, in part because this is a common theme in teacher complaint sessions and in part because there was no administrator present and in part because of the residual effect of the old faculty meetings in the Little Theatre. Maybe some teachers just felt emboldened to speak their mind in the very place where Ralph used to hold forth and they had always felt fearful of saying what they wanted to.

Sooner or later it was bound to happen. Tony Desista said it first. "You know, she's our leader, for christsake. Let's bring her back here. Let's bring the faculty meetings back to the Little Theatre, put the principal front and center, and hold her accountable. She's our leader and we want some answers."

"Here, here," from around the room.

Similar comments followed. A movement was born: let's return the faculty meetings to their rightful place, the Little Theatre—a place suited to confrontation, a place where a principal might be held accountable, a place where the line between teachers and administrators could be neatly drawn. The administrators would be there on the stage. The teachers would be here in the seats. The cafeteria was a dodge. There, the lines were obscured. Teachers and administrators sat together. Teachers faced teachers. Roles became confused, generalized. Who's accountable here anyway?

Good question.

Early in the 1980s, it seems, those unsympathetic to teachers saw accountability as a means of ensuring that those educator types would be kept in line and made to work. Some saw accountability as the price paid to the public in exchange for higher teacher salaries and greater professional autonomy. Sure, we'll give you all that money and freedom but we want results tomorrow and we're gonna hold you to it! Still others, Roberta Walters among them, saw accountability as a commodity that needed to be redistributed among school personnel. Her school management team was not just an effort to share the decision making but also a way of spreading around the burden of unpopular decisions. Holding faculty meetings in the cafeteria was a symbolic statement. It said we're not management and labor, we're a team.

Unfortunately, all the laws and regulations say we *are* management and labor. And try as she might, Roberta could not wish away the old order and simply declare a new one. Besides, it wasn't just laws and regulations. Roberta's efforts, and similar efforts by so many school principals during the 1980s to create collegiality and shared decision making, met up with opposition from teachers who simply did not want it. They liked the roles the way they were.

Gene Staedtler retired two years ago. Gene had been president of the Amesley Teachers Association for a good twenty years, right up to retirement. Gene's main passion as a union leader had been the professionalization of teachers, by which he meant freeing teachers from all responsibilities besides teaching in the classroom. No cafeteria duty, no hall duty, no study-hall supervision, no chaperoning dances, no homeroom, no filling in bubbles on computer sheets, no attendance keeping, no typing, no folding, duplicating, collating, mailing, or stamping. Teachers should be hired to teach, said Gene, and to employ them otherwise was not only professionally demeaning, it was a waste of tax dollars.

Consequently, Gene led the fight to eliminate cafeteria duty and to hire secretaries to type teacher tests, and as the result of two different collective bargaining agreements reached during his tenure as union president, had actually achieved these two modest but worthy goals.

I recently had a dream about Gene Staedtler. In my dream, Gene was holding forth in his classroom. He was not typing tests, nor was he collating and folding, nor was he doing any other nonteacherly task; he was delivering instruction. Only the periods were just seven minutes long, with forty-three minutes' passing time between. The real action was going on outside Gene's door in the hallway. In my dream, I must have been sitting at the rear of Gene's room because I could see Gene teaching up front and at the same time I could look through the window into the hallway. Gene was ebullient. There he was, drawing diagrams with circles and arrows on the board, parading back and forth across the front of the room as he gestured broadly at all the right moments in a nonstop lesson. At the end of seven minutes, the students rose from where they had been politely seated in columns and rows, moved unhurriedly toward the door, then joined spontaneously into the frenzy of music and movement in the corridor. Gene kept teaching. Eventually, after forty-three minutes had passed, the next group of students filed in, leaving behind the boisterousness of the hall, assuming instantly a polite attitude as they crossed the threshold and took their seats. Gene had not stopped teaching. There he was, marching to and fro, instructing with vigor, like a continuously running film loop, a thoroughly professionalized teacher.

In my dream Gene Staedtler gets his wish. It is the logical extreme of the traditional union view of teaching. The teacher, relieved of all managerial, secretarial, and custodial tasks, is finally free to teach, but is also out of touch. Not my vision of a vibrant profession. On the other hand, Roberta's wishful thinking, however well intended, might not lead us into the promised land either.

The Little Theatre movement lasted a few days. Shortly, Joe Grossi went back to cursing the copy machine for jamming—a more immediate concern. As for everybody else, the mob scene at the union meeting, rather than stirring up commitment, seemed, at least for the moment, to have just dulled their rage. The opposition thus spent itself.

As for Roberta Walters, she was starting to feel the heat. Her door, which in the fall had been mostly open, was now sometimes closed. I don't know if it was because there were secret conversations going on behind the closed doors or if she was seeking refuge. Either way, it was not a good sign.

One day I ran into Roberta in the student foyer. Our paths met and joined as we both headed down the ninth-grade hall. It was between periods and there was the usual crush of humanity, like a subway platform just after a train pulls up and opens its door. We were both in a hurry: I to class, Roberta to who knows where.

David Wheeden and Paul Murillo, both seniors, both large, and neither in any particular hurry, were ambling ahead of us. We were catching up fast. It soon became apparent why, or at least partly why, they were moving so slowly. David was kicking a spool of cash register tape, which unraveled as it tumbled along. There was, at that moment, a trail about twenty-five feet long.

Roberta bustled up alongside the boys and tapped Wheeden on the shoulder.

"Excuse me. David, right?"

"Yeah," said David.

"You know, you could just as easily pick that up as kick it along the floor," said Roberta.

David, keeping up with the flow, said, "I didn't drop it."

Roberta, bending to pick up the spool and pulling in its train, said, "Well, neither did I, but you see I'm bending to pick it up."

"That's the custodian's job," David answered. He glanced, I think nervously, at his principal, but hearing no reply kept going down the hall.

Roberta, with deepened commitment, gathered in the rest of the paper.

At this moment, the figure of Hal Murray, framed by the door of his science lab down the hall ahead of us, caught my eye. Hal had apparently watched this little encounter since at the moment I noticed him he was rolling his eyes and slapping hand to forehead in disbelief. Hal now stepped into the hall and grabbed David by the arm. Hal was going to make a statement, in both word and symbol.

"Wait a minute, David. That is your school principal who just spoke to you."

David, stunned by Mr. Murray's assertiveness, fell back to submissive mode. "Yes sir."

"Now don't you think you owe Mrs. Walters an apology?"

"Yes sir," said David. He hesitated.

"Well, come on. Let's go," Hal said.

Roberta and I had now reached David and Hal.

Murray spoke. "David wants to say something to you, Mrs. Walters."

David said, "I'm sorry."

Roberta said, "I'm just concerned that we all work together and do our part to make this school a real community. We all have to assume responsibility."

"Yes ma'am."

"You better get to class, David," Hal said. David left, and Murray turned to Walters. "You see, you just gotta be firm with these kids, Mrs. Walters." Roberta held her tongue.

Later that day, the story was repeated in the faculty room. "What a goddamned wimp," Hal said to Joe Grossi. "There're like these four or five seniors with these rolls of toilet paper. And as they're walking down the hall, they're kicking the rolls of toilet paper so they're unraveling. They must have been doing it from the student foyer 'cause the paper was stretched all the way, I mean *all* the way down the hall. Okay, so now guess who I see walking right behind them."

"Walters," Joe guesses.

"That's right. She's walking right behind them. Says absolutely nothing."

"Amazing."

"So finally I step in and I grab one of the kids and I give him a piece of my mind. So next, I look over and there's Walters and she's bending over picking up the paper, you know like one of those little guys with dustbins after the parade. So I take the kid by the arm. I bring him over to Walters and I tell him to apologize."

"What did Walters do?" asked Joe.

"She made some goddamned Milquetoasty remark like that's okay and don't do it again."

"And this is supposed to be the leader of our school," said Joe. Hal and Joe shook their heads.

Unfortunately, gossip is the chief mode of communication in an institution that makes no commitment to professional dialogue, that does not schedule regular opportunities for group planning and consultation. Consequently, interesting points of philosophical disagreement become polemical tales of sage versus fool in the embellished versions of faculty-room talk. Roberta sought to teach by example, by moral force. Hal chose a more direct method. You could make a case for either one, but all of that was lost in Hal's story.

The school management team next met on January 17. A low and brilliant winter sun streamed through the open venetian blinds in Conference Room A. All six team members were present, seated around the big square conference table. In addition to Bill Pierce, Roberta, and myself, there was Allen Perkins, science teacher and disciple of professional-duties-only Gene Staedtler. Then there was Ellie Grosshartig, a good twenty years in the classroom (home economics) and wise to the system but still enough of a sport to join a committee as a friendly gesture toward the new principal. And there was Bernice. Bernice Fleischmann, a mostly silent looming presence. Bernice of the spiked heels, erect posture, and trim business suits that looked military. When she chose to speak it was usually to note how present events were only further signs of the downfall of society and how it-wasn't-this-way-twenty-years-ago.

Roberta was upbeat. Contract negotiations, at impasse for a month, had just been concluded. Though the union and the board of education still had to ratify the agreement, word was that both parties would. Both sides were claiming victory in modest tones. For Roberta, this was the best kind of news. Now the rift that had opened between her and her faculty could be bridged. No longer would an us-them mentality endemic to labor-management relations dominate her dealings at the high school. Now the engine of school reform could begin to gather steam and start the slow chug-chug of real progress.

"Roberta, I'm sorry but I just think this whole thing is doomed to fail." Bill Pierce had just interrupted Roberta, who had been dreaming aloud with phrases like "school as community" and "the environment we create together."

"Look," said Bill, "there are basically two attitudes held by teachers in this school. One attitude says, I do my job in the classroom and the administrators take care of the rest. The other says, okay, we're all in this together and we've all gotta cooperate to make this school work. Unfortunately, there are a lot of people out there with the first attitude and as long as they're there, we're never going to have this romantic ideal that both you and I long for."

"Whadaya mean 'unfortunately'?" Allen Perkins asked.

"Whadaya mean 'romantic'?" Roberta said simultaneously.

Everybody laughed, which was a good thing because Allen and Roberta had just struck the heart of the matter.

"You go first," Roberta offered.

"Look," Allen said, "I went into teaching because I like science and because I like teaching kids. I did not go into it because I like hall duty or administration or guidance or figuring out the master schedule or coaching sports—or for that matter teaching biology, which I've had five sections of for the last five years. I'm an earth science teacher. That's what I like. That's what I do. Let the people who like all that other stuff do all the other stuff. Now you talk about the school as a community and everybody helping out. This school is not a community. It is an institution. Kids come here to learn. They don't come here to find themselves. So if you, the administrators, will do your job of keeping order in the hallways, then we teachers will be better able to do our job of giving instruction in the classrooms."

"Well, let's see. I'm not quite sure where to begin." Roberta paused thoughtfully. "Okay, Allen, I don't disagree with you. Kids come here to learn, or at least that's why we send them here. So learning is what schools are or should be all about. I think we agree there. Do we agree there?" Roberta looked at Allen, who nodded reluctantly; he was obviously uncomfortable with Roberta's socratic approach.

"Okay," Roberta continued, "what do we want them to learn?"

Allen interrupted, taking the bull by the horns. "We want them to learn math and science and English and social studies and all the rest. I mean, that's it, right?"

"Well, . . ." Roberta wanted to move slowly over this terrain. It was too well worn and the path that seemed to shoot straight as an arrow to the other side was, she believed, a deception. She seemed determined to make a careful inspection of the ground. "Okay," Roberta began again. "What you've just listed are subjects. Math and English and science and so on, right?"

"Yes, of course. Subjects." Allen was growing impatient.

"What is the content of those subjects?" Roberta asked.

"Give me a goddamned break. Come on, Roberta. I really don't see the point. I mean, I think it's all pretty straightforward and you're trying to make it complex. If you ask me, that's what educational theorizing always does, makes the simple complex. That's why ninety-five percent of it is useless anyway. Come on—math, English, phys ed, that's it. That's what we teach. What's so complicated about it?"

"Humor me, Allen." Roberta broke in. "Give me just another minute."

"Okay. I still haven't heard an answer to my question," Allen taunted.

Roberta looked across the table at Allen. "What is the content of those subjects?"

"Easy," said Allen, determined to prevail with his theme of simplicity. "In earth science it's rocks. In biology it's cells. Math, numbers. English, verbs. History, it's dates. Come on. I mean really. Isn't that what it's all about?" Allen looked around the table. Everybody looked at Roberta, apparently reserving judgment (except for Bernice, who clearly had already made up her mind about this conversation).

"Well," Roberta continued, "in each of those courses aren't there certain things beyond the verbs and the dates and the cells that we want kids to learn? Beyond all of that stuff, don't we really want kids to learn to think for themselves and to develop a desire to learn?"

Allen was knocked a little off balance. "Well, sure," he conceded, "but you can't really teach that. I mean you can't make that a part of the lesson plan. It either happens or it doesn't."

"That's precisely where we go wrong," said Roberta as if just coming to the realization herself. "That's it. That's my point, Allen. Those two things don't just happen. And they won't happen unless we figure out how to teach them. We all agree that the best thing we can do for our students is to get them to think for themselves and to develop a desire to learn on their own. I mean, we give at least lip service to those ideas, but when it comes to running schools, we get so bogged down in subjects and verbs and dates and rocks and cells, we lose sight of our real purpose."

"Roberta, please," Allen spoke, "don't misunderstand me. I couldn't agree with you more, but you're talking about some kind of an ideal world. And we don't have an ideal world. We have kids on drugs. Kids who don't want to be here. Kids who don't have any kind of a family. Kids who frankly—forgive the language—don't give a shit. And you're talking about inspiring them?!"

"That's right, Allen." If Allen could turn up the heat,

so could Roberta. "Now, let's think for a minute where this conversation began. We admit that our priority in schools as we know them is to teach subjects, right? Allen, that's what you answered when I asked. So, we organize schools to fit that purpose. We get teachers who teach subjects and we plug the kids into the subjects. We call that a schedule with five or six subjects a day, and because it's the subjects that matter, we don't think about the total environment that we create by making the subjects the priority. We all do our job, teaching subjects—or keeping order in the halls between subjects. Let's consider for a moment how we might do things differently if instead of making subjects the priority, we made getting kids to think and inspiring kids to be self-learners the priority."

Roberta and Allen had indeed touched the heart of one very important issue facing schools. What *is* our priority? If it is subjects, then what you see is what you get. That is the American high school. And while it can boast of a thick brochure of course offerings with exciting-sounding electives, it is probably not the best way to educate kids. With it we have created a kind of shopping mall where kids wander from one academic store to another, dabbling here and there without really gaining a coherent base of knowledge. This is what Arthur Powell talks about in *The Shopping Mall High School*, and it is as apt for Amesley as for most contemporary American high schools.[2] The focus is not, as it ought to be, on the mastery of certain essential skills over a period of several years; rather, the focus is the individual course, which may or may not have a meaningful relationship to other courses. Overarching goals, if there are any, are subservient to those courses. So, in what Theodore Sizer has called an atmosphere of "genial mindlessness," a student wanders the mall somewhat aimlessly, and once he or she has accumulated so many Carnegie units of course credit, a diploma is granted.[3]

And so we all thought for a minute, and then we talked some more, but the meeting's agenda was weighing heavily at hand so eventually we moved on, which is another one of our problems in public schools: we're kept so busy shoring up the old dykes, we never have a chance to step back and see

how we might otherwise keep back the sea. Because chaos
threatens regularly from all sides, reflection becomes a luxury.
However, ignoring it is a practice we can ill afford. Tide's up
and the old dykes just won't hold up much longer.

Allen, I am sure, remained unpersuaded, but perhaps
the tip of a wedge had been driven into his very untroubled
concept of schooling.

The new contract was ratified in February and everybody breathed a sigh of relief. Roberta still had big problems,
though. She wanted very much to move Amesley High School
away from the conventional mindlessness of American education toward something reconceived, with the right priorities.
But to do that, she had to win the trust and respect of the
faculty. And to do that she had to give them what they
thought they wanted: *order*. This was a real dilemma. To go
forward, she had to first go backward. And having once
moved backward, deeper into the viney embrace of conventional school wisdom, would she lose the chance of breaking
free? It would be a gamble.

Faculty meeting, April 6. Roberta was speaking.

"At our last meeting of the school management
team"—we had met twice since January 17—"we held a discussion on all the small distractions that keep you as teachers
from doing what you want to do and what you do best:
teach." This was well put, cast in just the sort of language
that would appeal to all the Allens in the room. "Here is the
list we came up with: Walkmans in the hallways and in the
classroom, smoking in the bathrooms, tardiness to class, eating in the hallways, and disrespectful language. It was felt by
the school management team that the sense of the faculty is
that we have to start chipping away at all these small discour-
tesies which over the years have been allowed to multiply. It
was agreed that if we came down hard all at once against all
these problems, there would probably be a student backlash.
So it was felt we should select, as a faculty, one of these problems and resolve to enforce the rule with consistency across
the board." I could tell that Roberta was uncomfortable with
this kind of "tough talk"—it wasn't her style—and at the

same time very pleased as she sensed her words resonating with the mood of the faculty. Or so she thought.

Joe Grossi, math teacher, raised his hand. "Well now wait a minute. All of those things that you just listed we already have rules for. The problem has been that when we write a kid up for breaking any of those rules, we don't get backed up by the administration. I say let's enforce them all, as we should have been doing all along anyway, as long as we can get a pledge right here and now that we'll get the kind of backup we need."

Roberta answered. "I have no problem with enforcing all of the rules and I would be willing to make that pledge right here and right now—"

"Then why don't you?" Joe interrupted.

"But I . . ." Roberta was trying to not break stride. "I just don't think that—"

George Handelman, assistant principal, sitting to her left, tapped Roberta on the arm. Roberta and George whispered back and forth. Roberta sat. George rose. A hush came over the room. George had been assistant to the last three principals. He had a reputation as a down-to-earth disciplinarian, and therefore had the respect of Joe and Allen and all like-minded individuals in the room.

"Let me elaborate on the answer Ms. Walters just gave from my perspective as the school disciplinarian, as it were." Ms. Walters hadn't really given an answer but that didn't seem to matter to George, who was simply trying to show solidarity with his boss.

"I, too, have no problem enforcing all the rules as long as everyone in this room lends equal support. But you know, the business of getting backed up works both ways. Case in point: yesterday a tenth-grader came into my office. She'd been written up for being late to homeroom. I asked her how many times she was late. She said once, and then launched into a thing about how her friend Mary or whatever didn't get written up until she was late five times because she has a different teacher, and how her friend Sue tells her she's late all the time and never gets written up 'cause her teacher

doesn't care. Now I don't necessarily believe every sob story
that a kid brings to my office, but I know, whether or not this
one is actually true, that kind of thing goes on. I think if
we're going to make any kind of pledging, and maybe that's
not a bad idea, we all need to work together."

Somehow the idea of let's-all-work-together sounded
more plausible when it came from George. George sat. The
room was quiet. We all knew that George was right. And we
knew that if we agreed to take on one of the "little distractions" mentioned by Roberta, the teachers would have to
police each other, a truly radical concept; radical because it
went against an unspoken rule that when confronted by a
situation involving a kid, a parent, or an administrator, one's
colleague is always right. Now we would have to criticize our
colleagues. Hey, Joe, how come you didn't write that kid up
for smoking in the bathroom? Hey, Bernice, I saw three kids
walk into your homeroom late yesterday. Comments like that,
which is what the future at Amesley now seemed to threaten,
could quickly undermine that deeply rooted pact of solidarity
that all teachers shared. No longer would the faculty room be
a safe haven for teachers seeking refuge from the battles raging everywhere else in the building. Even on that hallowed
ground, danger would be only as far away as the nearest colleague. Hey, Bill, I saw a kid walk right by you yesterday
carrying a soda can and you didn't say squat.

Anyway, George's remark had a sobering effect on the
faculty. Hal Murray tried valiantly to suggest that it was the
administration's responsibility to reprimand those teachers
who did not enforce school rules and that teachers should not
have to police each other. But Roberta suggested that would
not work since there are only two administrators and they
can't see everything that goes on in the building. So the idea
of policing each other seemed inevitable. I think the faculty
felt like they had fallen for a trap of their own making.

Shortly a vote was taken as to which of the "little distractions" everybody would resolve to work on, and Walkmans won out. So it was agreed that Walkmans would be
confiscated on sight and handed over to George Handelman

for the student to retrieve at the end of the month on the condition of pledging never to bring that Walkman or any similar Walkman to school again. And if a student refused to hand over a Walkman to a teacher, said student would be "written up" and yes, Roberta and George freely pledged, they would back the teachers up on this one. And so it became a done deal, a true case study in teacher empowerment, complete with shared decision making and voting and expanded teacher responsibility and teachers assuming ownership of the building and the administrators supporting the teachers and all the rest.

Thus we fell into the warm, familiar entangling embrace of conventional school wisdom. Create more rules, establish order, and a climate of respect will follow. Exactly backward. The ennui that characterizes so many middle-class kids in school is not addressed by rule making because lack of rules is not the root problem. Lack of purpose is. Our shopping mall high school, for all its sexy electives, has failed to get the attention of our students. Most see school as a slightly irrelevant necessity, irrelevant because they don't see the point.

What *is* the point? Ask the people in charge and you will get numerous answers. The contemporary high school is a product of all the political and social movements of the last century. It has weathered many political storms during that time and in the aftermath of each has taken on new roles and been assigned new tasks such that our mission is no longer clear. Ernest Boyer has written, "High schools have accumulated purposes like barnacles on a weathered ship."[4] Because there is pressure on schools to be all things to all people, we have become just that.[5]

The reformist wave of the 1980s is only the most recent layer of tasks and purposes. This time the driving force for school reform was economic competitiveness—keeping up not with the Soviets, as in the *sputnik* era, but the Japanese. The call went up early in the decade for simply more rigorous, tougher discipline. After all, that's how the Japanese educate their children. Witness the report of the National

Commission on Excellence in Education, *A Nation at Risk,* which warned in dire terms of a "rising tide of mediocrity."[6] Next, there appeared growing interest in Japanese management techniques: worker participation, site-based decision making, quality circles, and a general mood of rationalism, as though the simple application of scientifically validated teaching strategies would cure our ills.

Thus we arrive in the 1990s heavy laden with the baggage of a century of school reforms, much of it well intended, some of it successfully achieved, and all of it in some way still present in the form of regulations, mandated curricula, building architecture, and most important, the great confusion of attitudes both public and professional about what schools are supposed to be.

Not long after the faculty meeting, Joe Grossi and science teacher Mary North, an otherwise unlikely team, were discovered one day compiling a list of teacher names. Although the meaning of the list was never firmly established, a cloud of suspicion descended upon the two, who became known as the vice squad. To show it was all in good fun, they tacked up a "Wanted" poster on the back of the faculty lounge door with crudely drawn sketches of various teachers who had failed to enforce the new Walkman statute.

It was the kind of humor with a cutting edge since amidst all the laughter and playful accusation, Walkman confiscation became a regular thing. Indeed, one day shortly after the Most Wanted were posted, Mr. Nehring and Mr. Pierce, whose likenesses were included among the infamous, came barreling through the faculty lounge door giggling and holding aloft a Walkman, still warm and screaming with tunes. This act of atonement was met with snarls from the assembled teachers, who agreed that two more Walkmans must be snared before Nehring and Pierce could be crossed off the list. This was done, with flourish I might add, as the two teachers in question arranged for shop teacher Andy Wittenboom to provide three lacquered plaques on which their trophies could be mounted. The remaining Walkmans obtained, Nehring and Pierce ceremonially hung their mounted prizes (duplicates of the originals, which were ultimately returned) on the faculty lounge wall directly over the phone so that all would be reminded of their daring and vigilance.

For students, the new Walkman decree had the expected effect. On the whole the kids were unhappy. In the library I found a protest poem: "Roses are red / A Walkman's my right / Against this repression / The students will fight." But the fight never materialized. Besides the general moaning and verbal protests, there was no real show of student opposition, I think because enforcement was so universal. The kids knew they were licked. But I wasn't sure, so I decided to discuss the issue with my second-period global studies class.

"What do you think of the Walkman—"

"It sucks!"

"—ruling?"

"Why do you think the school made the rule?"

"Because teachers think the Walkmans disturb their lessons." This was Ray Slide, who also made the earlier comment.

"Well, that sounds like a pretty good reason, I think," I said.

Ray said, "Yeah, but we turn 'em off when class starts."

"Maybe *you* do, Ray, but not everybody else," I said.

"Oh yes we do, Mr. Nehring."

"Yeah."

"We always turn 'em off."

"You never have a problem with us." This from Nicky Martucci, whom I was always reminding to take her Walkman off.

"Well," I said, "I won't argue with you. But let's just suppose there were some teachers here at Amesley who had some students who frequently wore their Walkmans to class and who did not always voluntarily remove them as class started so that they became a regular imposition on the lesson. Would that not be a sound reason to make a rule that students may not bring their Walkmans altogether?"

"Mr. Nehring," said Nicky, "I really don't see the problem. I mean don't you think most kids take them off when class starts?"

"Most, yes," I answered.

"So then," Nicky continued, "all a teacher has to do is write up the kids who don't. I mean I really think sometimes teachers go overboard with rules. It's like they've gotta be in control all the time and they get paranoid when they think the littlest thing is gonna make them lose control."

This was a sound argument. In fact it was much like an argument Mr. Nehring had given at a recent faculty meeting.

"Okay, apart from the issue of control," I began, "can you think of any other reason why this rule should exist?"

A sampling of answers from around the room:

"Can't think of any."

"Nothing comes to mind."

"Not really."

"None."

"Well, let me put it another way," I said.

"Sounds like a good idea, Mr. Nehring," said Ray.

"Let's suppose," I said, "that one afternoon you're feeling kind of moody and reflective."

"Moody and reflective, Mr. Nehring?" said Ray.

"Okay, Ray, pissed off at the world." I recognized instantly that I shouldn't have made this very appropriate remark. "Anyway, you put on your favorite tape of your favorite band and there's one song in particular you want to listen to and you really want to listen to the words and think about them. You with me?"

The class nodded.

"So you listen to this song and it really fits your mood and the words are just right for whatever it is you're upset about and you're really thinking about the words and the song is making you feel better and it sets you to thinking about how you might deal with your troubles and all of a sudden the song ends and the next cut on the album starts up and it's loud and a completely different mood and it's ruining your good feeling and your train of thought. What are you gonna do?"

"Turn it off," said Amy.

"Good," I said. "Now let's suppose your math teacher has just gone through an elaborate math problem. And she's just spent the last fifteen minutes of class setting it up and getting your interest and getting you to think about it and all of a sudden the bell rings. What do you think she hopes you will do as you gather up your things and get up out of your seat?"

"Leave," said Ray.

"Okay, wiseguy, but as you are leaving what do you think she hopes you will be thinking about?"

"The math problem, Mr. Nehring," said Alice.

"Right," I said. "Now if your school doesn't have a rule against Walkmans, what might people be tempted to do even if they have some interest in the math problem?"

"They might listen to their Walkman, Mr. Nehring," said Ray mechanically.

"Yeah, but Mr. Nehring." This was Jenna, until now silent. "It's the school's fault to start with. I mean they rang the bell and made us leave and like if they thought our math teacher's problem was really cool, why don't they just let us stay?"

"Yeah, that's right," added Jason. "All we're gonna do is like go off to English class and do verbs and forget about the math problem."

"Yeah, or biology and do cells."

"Yeah, or social studies and do more dates."

2.

It's a Great Plan,
But It'll Never Work

It's hard sometimes to argue with my students because sometimes they're right. They see through the contradictions of the system, even though they are capable of a few contradictions themselves. Their actions and occasionally their words compel us more than any education report to rethink what schools are about. That's why when Bill Pierce showed me the grant application in April of the year Ralph Peters left (Roberta Walters was to arrive that fall), I thought it looked pretty neat.

"Look, Jim," I remember Bill saying, "here's our chance to really bring on the revolution now that Mao is gone." Mao Zedong is what Bill called Ralph. "And they'll pay us to do it." It seems the state education department was offering competitive grants to schools for summer seminars. The idea was that school personnel would design some kind of self-education project that was group oriented and would be completed over the course of one week during the summer. The participants would get $100 a day for their efforts, which, Bill was quick to add, did not have to result in any kind of a real program. The whole purpose of the grant project, Bill pointed out, was to get teachers working together, and so if we just dreamed up some kind of thing where we would all just sit around and talk and drink coffee and act "collegial" without really having to make something of it, that's exactly what they were looking for. Bill said it was the best scam to come our way in years.

Bill Pierce and I had been friends ever since I started teaching at Amesley ten years before. That first year he'd helped me out with a big rowdy last-period class of ninth-graders, and ever since our bond of friendship had grown through numerous mutual trials and misadventures. I occasionally helped Bill with the literary arts magazine (always a lightning rod to controversy), and we'd sat together on more committees than either of us would want to remember. I liked Bill because deep down he really cared about kids and he really enjoyed working with them. He affected a cavalier style (like calling the grant a scam) that sometimes got him in trouble, but I think it was his way of saying I know who I am so I don't need to impress you.

At any rate, the prospect of a summer free of house painting—the way Bill and I kept from going broke most summers—was good incentive, and the idea that somebody was willing to pay a bunch of teachers to use their minds was truly novel. So Bill and I got together one Saturday morning and wrote up our Professional Access to Excellence grant application. The idea basically was to get together seven or eight high school people—teachers, counselors, administrators—and design the ideal high school. Having been tipped off that the new assistant commissioner who would be reading the applications was into "grass roots initiatives" and "collegial interaction" and "mutual self-support networking" and "team-based program strategies," we made sure our application was well seasoned with such esteemed language. Bill and I agreed at about 3:00 P.M. that Saturday as we signed our names in four places, including one on the margin for "file access feasibility," that this here grant application caught the true spirit of the program's intent and that being so neatly composed and carefully thought through, it would rise quickly to the top of the stack.

But it did not rise high enough. At the end of May, Bill received in his school mailbox a "due-to-the-large-number-of-outstanding-applications" letter. We resolved shortly thereafter to take only jobs where we could use latex paints. Turpentine was messy and took too long. After five years in the business, we figured we could be somewhat discriminating. And after all it had been true presumption for a couple of teachers to think they could squander away taxpayer dollars lounging around and thinking during the summer months when they should be out house painting, even if it was all funded by an official Professional Access to Excellence grant.

Then one day in mid-June, Bill found another envelope in his mailbox with the same official state education department markings. Bill waited for me, and we opened it together. Inside was a check made out jointly to William J. Pierce and the Amesley Central School District in the amount of $3,850.03, the exact (and quite arbitrary) amount we had requested. There was no letter attached. But in the lower left corner of the check where it says "memo" were the words *Professional Access to Excellence.* Our PAE money had come through after all.

We immediately informed the other five individuals named in our application: George Handelman, assistant principal; Mary North, biology teacher; Bob Reynolds, guidance counselor; Ellie Grosshartig, home economics teacher; and Jerry Rubicon, social studies teacher and chief negotiator for the union. At $100 a day times seven people times five days, you get $3,500; we had added $350.03 for books and supplies. When we informed our fellow awardees, most of them seemed stunned; I think they had never expected the application would succeed and were really just doing Nehring and Pierce a favor by allowing their names to be included. Indeed, there had been numerous individuals who had declined our offer of summer employment back when we were writing the application. Ultimately, the five got used to the idea that our little project was actually coming to pass. After all, it was only a week and it *was* $500, and having once said yes they couldn't very well back out now.

Next, Bill and I threw out our original grant application and sat down to figure out what we would really do with seven people for one week. We asked ourselves what really had motivated us to write this grant. Besides a strong desire to escape house painting, we decided, it was a desire to think together reflectively about our work with kids—which after all was the goal of the grant program, so whatever bureaucratic snafu led to our receiving the check was truly just and divinely directed. All the hefty education reports authored by big shots were just fine, but what kind of a report might be generated by a group of practitioners if you gave them the time and money, and more important the implicit vote of confidence that those two things carry, to write their own report? We decided that our week of collegiality would culminate in a document, our credo. Maybe not The Solution to the ills of education everywhere, but simply what we ourselves would do, how we might reorganize our high school, using existing resources to best serve kids. A credo made manifest in the vision of our ideal school.

One good thing that came out of the school reform discussions of the 1980s was the notion that teachers ought to have more say about what goes on in schools, not because we need to be nicer to teachers, but because teachers have an impressive experiential base of knowledge about kids. Unfortunately, the way schools are organized, and the way a teacher's job is defined, there is very little opportunity for a teacher to reflect on that impressive experiential base of knowledge and really consider how schools might be made better.

What's more, the way we educate future teachers in this country does little to equip teachers with the kind of skills necessary to renew schools. John Goodlad concluded in 1990, at the end of a five-year nationwide study of teacher education, that education programs equip future teachers not to renew a worn-out system but rather to adjust to it and fit in.[1] This, he says, is because teacher education has lost sight of its primary mission (to train teachers) and has been sucked into the reward system of higher education, which values research over teaching. Thus the focus of energy in colleges and departments of education has become research *about* schools rather than service *to* them through quality teacher-training programs. Also, for most colleges and universities, teacher education is a low-priority budget item.

That it is a low priority within the university reflects, I think, a larger societal attitude: having really good teachers in public schools is not and never has been a high priority. Why? Historically, teaching has been a woman's profession, associated with motherhood (esteemed but not valued); historically, also, public schools have served the middle and lower classes, not our future leaders; and, fundamentally, there is an unspoken rationale that says that since so much of schooling is just crowd control and keeping order, we really don't need highly skilled professionals. All we really need is warm bodies with gruff voices.

Given all that, it was truly encouraging to hear during the 1980s that we ought to listen more to teachers and let them take a hand in reshaping schools. That's what the PAE grant was all about. It was a chance for teachers to relent from merely perpetuating the system and become involved in reshaping it.

"Who is Credo?" asked George Handelman, caressing with his right hand his first cup of coffee of the day on Monday, July 19, at 8:15 in the morning. It was day one of our week of PAE grant seminars. He held in his left hand a one-page overview for the week ahead that Bill and I had put together. All seven of us were gathered in Conference Room 2. If a stranger had walked into the room it would have been very clear who was leading this group. Bill and I stood together at one end of the table nervous and animated, the others lounged in chairs sleepily, almost smugly. Bill and I had the bearing of two guys under the gun, which we were.

Despite our best efforts to keep a low profile to our PAE project, the superintendent of schools, Dr. O. J. David McBrave, had trumpeted our dubious success in the "Have

You Heard" section in the June issue of the *Amesley Crier*, our district newsletter. The story was then picked up by Amesley's own community newspaper, the *Post-Herald Daily*, which reported that Mr. William Pierce and Mr. James Nehring had been given $38,500.30 to develop plans for a new high school. O. J. Dave then called to say that State Ed wanted to verify the amount of our grant. We confirmed the real amount and then heard nothing further, fearing all the while that State Ed would pull our grant and we would be back to house painting, our credibility as educational leaders forever blackened. (Worse things, we conceded, could happen.)

Having been propelled by such events to the first morning of our state-sponsored collegiality project, we were feeling the full weight of our responsibility. Our colleagues and now the community were watching.

"Well, George," I said, "it's Latin for belief, meaning our belief about how we think the schools ought to be."

"I say drop it," says Ellie. "As I see it, what we're trying to do here is figure out what we would do if we ran the school. Let's save the Latin for university reports.

"Okay now," Ellie continued. "Basically, what you're saying to us here"—Ellie looked at the handout—"is you want us to all spend two days designing our ideal high school, then two days writing it up and finally one day where we talk about how we're going to implement it. Is that it?"

"Basically," I said.

"Hey, what the hell, Ellie," said Bill, "that's not too much for one week."

"Why stop with the high school?" Bob Reynolds, guidance counselor, charged in. "We'll do the rest of the school district in the afternoons."

Everyone laughed. I think George Handelman regarded me as a flake, and the Latin just confirmed this for him. Ellie and Bob were good sports but were annoyed that we had been awarded the grant. So, they figured, Bill and I were due some abuse.

Fitfully, our little project chugged, sputtered, and

lurched forward. That first day was spent mostly getting to
feel comfortable as co-workers, as a group. There was a lot of
moaning about the sorry state of Amesley High School and
of high schools in general, and there was a fair amount of
black humor about kids. We agreed, for example, that our
model school would have, not a dropout prevention counselor as Amesley was planning, but rather a dropout encour-
agement counselor. This led to a discussion of all the different
kinds of professional support people we now have in school:
psychologists, reading specialists, social workers, dropout prevention counselors, guidance counselors (Bob protested
including this one in the list but was outvoted), administrators (George protested), and substance abuse counselors. We
decided to count up just how many adults worked in our
building. George dug up the personnel list. We argued
whether we should count the teaching aides and custodians
and decided that, as important as they were, we'd just count
the professional educators—teachers, administrators, counselors of all kinds. Eighty-two.

"George," I asked, "how many kids go to Amesley
High School?"

"When I did the end-of-the-year summary sheets in
June, I think the number was something like one thousand
and fifty-six, something like that."

"Okay," I said. "Ah, let's see. Um, we'll do some
math." I stood at the board working long division: one thousand fifty-six divided by eighty-two. Everybody watched,
which made me nervous. Mary, the science teacher, said my
columns were sloppy, which didn't help.

"Okay, I get something like twelve-point-eight. Rough-
ly thirteen kids. That means—think about this a minute
guys—for every professional in this school there are thirteen
kids. A one to thirteen ratio. Imagine teaching thirteen kids.
Bill, how many students did you have this year?"

"One hundred twenty-seven. Read 'em and weep."

"Jerry?"

"I don't know. A hundred, hundred and fifty? With
eighth-graders, anything over ten I stop counting."

"That's incredible. You all have over a hundred students, which means—"

Bob interrupted. "What about me? You gonna count the poor guidance counselor?"

"Sure, Bob," I said. "I was just going to say, what about Bob Reynolds."

"I've got three hundred and fifty-two kids that I'm responsible for."

"God," Jerry moaned.

"Including eighth-graders," Bob added.

Now George interrupted. "Hey, you gonna count me in all this?"

"Sure, George," I said. "Anybody can play, it's easy."

"Well," George began, "I'm responsible for disciplining all one thousand fifty-six of those little monsters that you all teach, and I see about thirty every morning for all those referral slips you so generously send down to my office each day."

"George, only thirty? I'll stop exercising restraint," I said. "Okay, our little calculation on the board shows that here at Amesley Junior-Senior High School with one thousand fifty-six kids and eighty-two educators, we have a sort of a raw student-to-educator ratio of about thirteen to one, give or take point-two kids, yet the way we've chosen to organize things around here, we've got teachers meeting with a hundred ten or a hundred twenty kids in a day and guidance counselors responsible for three hundred fifty, and George gets to discipline the whole slew of 'em. You know, this really does not make sense. I mean, it's like we have the resources to make education pretty good but we choose instead to see how we can manipulate an essentially good student-teacher ratio to make it work in the least productive way."

Though much of our first day had been spent spinning our wheels, a necessary but frustrating process, at day's end the reality of these numbers struck us all. The light they shed cast a long beam down the length of our week of meetings, ultimately granting us a new vision—no, granting us a vision where previously there had been none—of what a good school might really look like. We left Conference Room 2 on Monday afternoon genuinely excited about our work.

A one to thirteen ratio. That's the ratio you'll find in many schools. Pretty attractive numbers. So how come a high school teacher meets with maybe 120 kids each day? Because of specialization. Over the years, we teachers have allowed our own perception of what we are capable of teaching to be diminished. Teachers in one-room schoolhouses taught all subjects. Now, almost without exception we are departmentalized into math, science, English, and so on. Even within departments we often stake out turf: Roger is our American history person, Nicky knows sociology and psychology. Like that.

Of course comparison with one-room schools is not entirely fair, since student aspirations and course sophistication were not what they are in the contemporary comprehensive high school. Still, I believe we've become more specialized than is either necessary or educationally sound.

Why have teachers become so highly specialized? First, because of increasing pressure during the last century both within teaching and from the general public to raise professional standards, to increase expertise with subject matter; second, new areas of specialization and certification (for example, special education, which resulted from legislation in the 1960s and 1970s); third, the increasing centralization of schools during the last thirty years has increased enrollments and staffing, allowing departments the luxury of maintaining subspecialists. Thus have we become a very specialized profession. There are admittedly good reasons, but in so doing we have heaped upon ourselves huge numbers of students. Our committee was going to try to change that, to reverse the specialization trend.

"So wait a minute, you're saying I'm going to counsel kids, teach science, *and* be an administrator?" Mary asked incredulously. It was Tuesday morning and we were talking about an idea that Bill had come up with Monday evening.

"Well, I thought maybe you'd cover a little math, too," said Bill.

"Very funny," said Mary.

Our model school, or at least Bill's nascent concept of it, was running up against its first obstacle—us, and our very limited view of what each of us was capable of doing. Bill's idea went like this: take eighty kids and six educators with varied expertise, give them a secretary and an aide, place them in adequate space, a portion of the school building consisting of several rooms, and allow to simmer without stirring for four years.

"Think of it like Volvos, how they build Volvos," said Bill.

"Like Volvos?" Ellie asked.

"I like the recipe concept better," Bob said.

"Volvos," said Bill.

"You're serious," said George.

"I'm serious."

Mary said, "Well, my brother had a Volvo once. He said it was a great car. I don't know how they build 'em, though; I guess the way they build most cars."

"How do they build most cars?" Bill asked.

"I know how they build Volvos," said Jerry. "I used to have one. They take great pride in their methods."

"Go ahead, Jerry," said Bill.

"Well, for most cars, there's an assembly line. The cars roll along and get built from the ground up. As each car comes down the line, different people fasten on different parts, so each worker does the same routine task all day long. At Volvo, what they do is they have the assembly line, except that a team of maybe a dozen people builds the whole car. In other words, one group of people builds each individual car. They put together the chassis, then they all go to the mechanical shop and put in the engine, then they all go to the body shop and construct the body and so on."

"That's right," said Bill. "Okay, now I want to make an analogy. The way we've set up schools is like the typical assembly line. Each worker fastens on a part: each teacher fastens on a subject. Then on rolls the car or the kid to the next fastener. What I propose is that, instead, we work as teams. Each team takes exclusive responsibility for a group of students, takes them through their high school years from start to finish. For the same reasons that it works in industry, it'll work with us."

"What reasons are those?" Bob asked skeptically.

"Okay, reasons." Bill paused to think. "First, teachers see the whole kid. They come to know him or her as an individual, not just that student in the third row. Also, the team feels a greater sense of responsibility, a bigger stake in the success of the child because that success is in their hands; no other teachers are involved. Also, the teachers can feel freer to tinker with the curriculum and with teaching strategies because they don't have to worry about the next teacher along the assembly line saying, Hey this kid isn't properly fitted. Thus, they can alter their methods to suit their group of kids. As for the kids, they'll start to feel like a part of a community instead of just being passed from one teacher to the next all day long year after year. There will be some stability, some sense that the adults in their lives will be there. I think you'll see a lot less alienation, a lot less smoking in the boys' room and spray-paint-the-walls kind of problems. I mean, that's basically the idea. I think it could work."

There has been *some* beneficial fallout from all the school reform talk of the 1980s. Part of it has been a renewed interest in team teaching. This very worthy idea has been a regular feature of school-reform proposals stretching back to John Dewey but has never quite managed to become a regular part of the system because it goes against established norms of specialization and individualism (because teachers are accustomed to teaching by themselves). The question is, can we get the idea to stick this time around? Maybe, since this time teaming is not just an idea being tried out in education. It's being tried in American industry, too. And since the organization of public education has traditionally taken its cue from industrial organization, there's hope. Besides, Japanese industry uses teams.

'What I didn't tell you," said Jerry, breaking the silence

that followed Bill's oration, "is my Volvo was always breaking down."

All day Tuesday we hashed over Bill's idea. How could
you possibly teach all those subjects with just six teachers?
Answer: you couldn't; instead the goal would be getting kids
to think more deeply about fewer subjects. Wouldn't you still
have to have an overall school administrator for discipline
and guidance counselors and so on in addition to these teams?
Answer: no; the teams would be responsible for everything—
instruction, scheduling, guidance, discipline. Wouldn't you
meet up with a lot of resistance from faculty and members of
the community? Answer: yes. And that would be your greatest
obstacle.

Resistance is always an issue, especially in a public
school with a core of teachers who've been around a while.
They've seen it all. And *innovation* is a word that makes some
veteran teachers justifiably nervous. Consider the following.

Some years ago, a new superintendent arrived at Amesley. He stayed just two years but in that time managed to
generate more ill will among the teaching staff than anyone
before or since. He wanted to make some changes. His angle
was "the parent connection," as he put it, and he cited "a
growing body of research" (also his words) clearly indicating
that when contact is made between parent and teacher early
in the school year, and is maintained during the school year,
student achievement rises. Amesley achievement scores had
been in a slump for several years, so when Dr. Alfonse T.
Biemer came into town on his white steed quoting research,
the board of education no doubt concluded this was the man
for them.

Charge!

"And to show our commitment to kids, I'm going to
challenge each of us to make some kind of personal contact
with the parents of each of our students by the beginning of
October. It may be just a simple phone call or a personal note
in the mail, but if we all resolve now to do it, I give you my
personal guarantee that it will start a quiet revolution that
will turn the Amesley schools around." Thus spake Alfonse

at the opening faculty meeting of the school year. I don't think the assembled teachers appreciated the literalness with which Dr. Biemer spoke that day. I think it registered as just background noise, an indistinct segment of the expected and enduring glom of opening-day speeches. The memo, however, registered. It arrived in everybody's mailboxes on the fourth day of school just as the full weight of school responsibilities was nestling into its usual spot between neck and shoulder blades.

"Is this guy for real? Every kid by the beginning of October?!"

"Looks like."

"What do we leave out? Going to the bathroom?"

"Same bullshit every year. Do more. Do more."

"Why is it that innovation always means finding new ways for overworked teachers to do more work?"

Shortly, the teachers called on Jerry Rubicon to intervene. Surely Jerry, with all his experience in contract negotiations, could set this guy straight.

Mr. Rubicon and Dr. Biemer met. Mr. Rubicon came away shaking his head. "The man can do it," said Jerry. "He's fully within his rights as our supervisor. There is nothing in the contract that says he can't."

"How about common sense?" someone asked.

"Unfortunately," said Jerry, "our relationship with the school district is not based on that."

Thus commenced a great flurry of typically neurotic school activity as teachers attempted to meet the deadline. Making phone calls from school became impossible; the only three phones available to teachers were in constant use. School stationery ran out after the second week. Dr. Biemer insisted that our "personal contact" could not be made via the standard progress report forms, which by the way we were expected to use for all students in addition to making the "personal contact" with mom and dad.

At the beginning of October, the deadline, which even Dr. Biemer had enough common sense to realize was ludicrous, was extended by two weeks. The memo that brought this cheerful news also announced Dr. Biemer's latest challenge: "visit the home of at least five of our students before the end of the first semester." Clearly, the additional two weeks gave us enough free time to make home visits, and, Dr. Biemer's memo reminded us, he was fully committed to that growing body of research. Joe Grossi remarked that Dr. Biemer should be fully committed, period.

Jerry Rubicon was able to get some movement on the home visitation directive since it implied after-school time, thus lengthening the school day, very much a contract issue. Biemer back stepped and indicated in his next memo that while home visitation was an excellent concept and most teachers were presently doing it anyway, his earlier directive had really been meant as a kind of a pat on the back and a reminder that a teacher might possibly and very optionally try home visits if he or she was not already doing so.

Over the course of the next year and a half, Dr. Alfonse T. Biemer kept up a steady stream of "innovative ideas" designed to increase parent-teacher contact. He encouraged participation in the PTA, a nice enough idea in itself, except that he made note of which teachers attended meetings. He encouraged parents to visit school during the day, which they did at the elementary school, but at the high school I think I saw one parent fearfully treading the halls one morning, and that was it. And the once-yearly back-to-school night became twice yearly.

At the end of his second year, Dr. Biemer left the Amesley School District a frustrated man. I suspect he felt very bitter toward the teaching staff, regarding them as wimpish and stubborn, afraid of innovation and progress. As for the teaching staff, the Biemer regime unfortunately only confirmed that growing body of experience that said innovation means someone else's faddish idea and more work for us.

"I become suspect," said Mary, rising from her chair to stretch, "when I hear words like *innovation* because it always comes down to more work for teachers. I mean that's always the bottom line." Our PAE committee was getting down to fundamental issues.

"But," I said, "if every change that comes down the line is suspect, how do schools change?"

"They don't," said Jerry flatly.

"How about *our* plan?" said Bill. "I mean the one we're working with here? Is it just more work for teachers? We're talking about teachers doing guidance and administration."

"Sounds like more work," said Mary.

"Well, wait a minute," Bill continued. "We've actually reduced the number of students that a teacher works with from say a hundred and thirty to eighty. And we're giving that teacher the services of two assistants. Now we've done that without adding staff or increasing any other resources, and we've brought the pupil load dramatically down for the individual teacher."

"With eighty kids, though, you're still gonna be meeting with at least four classes," said Mary.

"If you use a conventional schedule," said Bill. "We're too used to thinking of the school day as an eight-part series of forty-five-minute episodes. Why does it have to be that way? Couldn't we do something else?"

We could. A story:

Every year, I take a group of students from Amesley to a school in a nearby county where a Model United Nations Conference is held. There, about three hundred high school kids participate in a full-blown simulation of the United Nations. They meet in committees (international terrorism, environmental protection, world health), propose and debate resolutions, and meet in general assembly. The conference is planned and carried out in its entirety by kids. There are no periods. There are no bells. And committees regularly adjourn later than planned.

The chairperson for the committee on military security rapped his gavel and barked for order among the forty-odd delegates, who were all talking at the same time. The gavel worked. There was momentary silence, and the chairperson spoke.

"We have a motion to go to a vote. We have heard arguments pro and con, we've gone through general debate, we've adopted a friendly amendment, and we're asking now if there is a second to the motion." Everyone settled back into their seats. Order was restored.

The committee was now ready to adopt Lebanon's resolution calling for withdrawal of foreign military forces. With some luck, the resolution might be brought before the general assembly the following afternoon and, if successfully defended, be approved as the official position of the United Nations—or a kids' version of it anyway.

"Will the debate from the United Kingdom please make his comment in the form of a question?" It's Friday night with the international terrorism committee.

The delegate answers, "Oh come on, you guys. You're so goddamn caught up in protocol, you've lost sight of our purpose here. We're not—"

The chair raps his gavel. "Procedure requires that during time designated for questioning, only *questions* may be asked. Now, will the delegate from the United Kingdom kindly make his comment in the form of a question?"

"Oh, hell, a question. Okay. *Does* the delegate from Norway really believe that . . ."

The chair, a tall boy in tie and jacket, is exercising official authority for possibly the first time in his life—an important moment. The representative from the United Kingdom, also tall but with open flannel shirt and blue jeans, is learning that protocol is not just an artifice of the adult world but, judging by the unamused stares of his peers, something valued by people his own age learning the processes of institutionalized power.

"This is so incredibly frustrating." The delegate from Argentina with feather earrings and a rock and roll T-shirt shook her head as she talked with the delegate from Lebanon in the lobby between sessions. "I mean we just sit there and debate endlessly over some fine point of wording. I mean this one kid, the Soviet Union, kept insisting that our resolution should read 'and' instead of 'or' and it really didn't matter. And the United States kept contradicting everything he said. I think we've passed maybe one resolution in committee after six hours of debate. It's ridiculous." Argentina was learning that any process of shared power is slow and inefficient, and that it requires patience and tolerance. The manner in which she learned it, six hours of firsthand torture, had certainly affected her soul more deeply and enduringly than a semester of classroom instruction ever could.

It was 3:45 in the afternoon, the second day of the UN conference. Thirty weary delegates to the committee on environmental protection were struggling toward adopting Canada's resolution on acid rain. If they were to bring anything to the general assembly, scheduled to convene at 4:00, they would have to act now. But progress was blocked by a proposed amendment.

"Listen, if you agree to accept Sweden's change in your resolution as a friendly amendment, all the Scandinavian countries will support the resolution." The chairperson of the committee leaned toward the delegate from Canada and pointed to the Scandinavian delegates, who were all nodding their heads hopefully. Canada looked at the Scandinavians. She looked at the chairperson. And nervously back at the Scandinavians. "I don't know," she said. Everybody on the committee groaned. "Okay, okay, I accept," she said. The chairperson clicked his pen, openly proud of a successfully brokered compromise. A charge of energy shot through the entire committee from a sense that they were witnessing and taking part in a process they'd often been taught about in their social studies classes but never experienced. Now they were the important decision-making body, even if it was only a game.

That UN conference is a source of inspiration for me. It says there is at least *one* way to structure learning other than an eight-period day of teacher lectures. And there are others still: the school play, school music groups, athletic teams, the school newspaper, community internships, independent study. Wait a minute, aren't we already doing all of this? Yes, we are, but, ironically, it all occurs on the periphery of school life. This list represents some of the best, most active learning that kids engage in. Very little of it involves lecture, and a good deal of it occurs outside the conventional class-room and outside a forty-five-minute period. It's time school people learn some lessons. It's time to give serious thought to alternate ways of structuring school activity. That's what our PAE project was all about.

Back in Conference Room 2, the seven of us wearily looked across the table at each other. The table was littered with papers, used-up sugar packets, and coffee stirrers. It was late, and we were feeling beaten. Bill had challenged us to imagine something other than the schools we know. But our imagination was blunted by the fact that all the schools any of us had ever known were essentially the same. The great monolith of American public education, though very much a social construct, loomed large and imposing like a force of nature. Its routines and commonalities seemed a fixed part of the American landscape like the Great Plains and the Rocky Mountains and the Grand Canyon. Chalk and rulers, bells and subjects, grades and tests, passing and failing, English, then math, then science, then gym. Huckleberry Finn and square roots and mitochondria and medicine ball. Examples of something fundamentally different, like a model UN con-ference, were few and far between. We adjourned Tuesday with a collective feeling of imaginative barrenness.

A night's rest did us all good.

We spent most of Wednesday morning making up alter-native schedules and listing special group projects for our model school. By noon, I think we were starting to believe we had a plan that might actually work, or at least a plan we could write up into a report to justify our PAE grant. Bill Pierce was chief editor since the idea was essentially his. The rest of us each wrote a section. Dr. McBrave had advised us in a memo several weeks earlier that whatever sort of a plan we came up with, it should be based on existing resources of personnel and money. In the memo, he'd talked about how "budget formulation" and "district demographics" do not suggest "vast new monies in the foreseeable future." Also that "replication of viable pilot programs must be predicated on per-pupil expenditures not exceeding regular school outlays." All of which meant that O. J. Dave didn't want any of this to cost anything. Jerry Rubicon had a problem with that.

"They'll bleed you cold every time," Jerry said when it had come up Monday afternoon.

"You got that right," said Mary.

Jerry continued. "You have to accept as a basic premise that if you want a school district on the cutting edge, if you want to have innovative programs, you've gotta spend a little do-re-mi. But this administration does not see it that way. It's short-sighted management. They figure they can exploit their teachers, soak up their creativity and good will, then pat 'em on the back, say thank you very much and not spend one red cent. And people ask why teacher burnout is so high."

"You're right, Jerry, but—" Bill started.

"Damn straight I'm right," Jerry interrupted. Bill and Jerry didn't always see eye to eye.

"But . . ." Bill repeated and paused.

"Yeah, Pierce. We're listening," said Jerry with Cheshire smile.

"How many special programs have we seen go by the wayside because they cost too much money? I can think of three in just the last fifteen years or so which started out with tremendous enthusiasm and really seemed to be working, but over the years funding slowly got pulled, the program eroded, and eventually there was nothing left. I mean, look at the gifted and talented program that Janet started, what, ten years ago? Classes had like fifteen kids, they had a budget for field trips, it was great. But what happened? Classes mysteriously got bigger and the budget mysteriously got smaller and eventually there was no budget at all. My point is this: if we go ahead and design our little model here and it's got a big price tag, we may see it go into place, but instead of catching on and spreading, it'll go the way of all the other pricy innovations that have come and gone."

"So what you're saying is, we give in to the status quo," said Jerry.

"What I'm saying is," said Bill, "we think practically and politically."

"There's another side to this," said Bob. "Let's suppose we design this model high school and by some stroke of incredible luck we get a chance to try it out. Let's also suppose that we meet with some success: the kids like it, the community supports it, the teachers are gung-ho. If we've gone the pricy route with big budgets and special dispensations, then you know what everyone will say about our success. They'll say, oh, of course your project succeeded. If you gave me that kind of money, I could succeed, too. Right? Won't people say that?"

"They might think it," Jerry conceded.

"Now suppose," Bob continued, "we put a project in place that cost no more than all the other regular school programs, and then suppose we meet with a little success, our critics have all the wind taken out of their sails."

"They'll think of something. They always do." This was Jerry's way of admitting Bob made sense.

Our discussion was reaching down to the hard bedrock of school-reform issues. Fundamental was money, and the question of spend-more-to-do-better or do-better-with-what-you've-got. Lack of money, in a suburban district like Amesley, is *not* the main problem. In fact, looking at the national picture, the United States compares favorably with other industrial nations for school expenditures as a percentage of gross national product.[2] We *can* do better with what we've got, not by working harder but, to borrow the old IBM slogan, by working smarter. We might start by leveling the towering administrative bureaucracies that siphon off dollars before they get to the classroom, particularly in cities.

In the course of Tuesday and Wednesday the great schism over funding was bridged when someone offered a compromise: whatever program we came up with, it would be designed to cost no more than the standard per-pupil expenditure for the district, but we would allow for startup costs over and above that for special training, curriculum writing, and so on. Jerry said he could live with that.

Once we'd settled that issue, writing the report turned out to be fairly easy. By the end of the day on Thursday, we had a working draft, which Bill agreed to polish up later in the summer. Friday was reserved for a discussion of implementation. How would we get this thing from paper into practice?

"Good luck!"

"Pipe dream."

The general tone of Friday was that we'd done our part. We'd written a fine report, and now it was up to those administrators to do something with it.

Every now and then, I play a game with my ninth-graders. I call it Silence Is Golden after my own eighth-grade teacher who often said, "Silence is golden, but gold is rare." It usually goes like this.

It's last period. A big class. A big rowdy class. I've struggled all period just to keep the kids in their seats. Now as the second hand starts its final sweep to meet the big twelve at 2:30, my kids are like race horses frothing at the starting gate. I'm trying to give some last-minute direction about pages for homework. Nobody is listening. I mean *nobody*. So I say, "Okay, guys, nobody gets out of here alive until everybody is quiet for ten seconds." Nobody hears, of course. So I just stand there. Nobody notices. So I sit down and start shuffling papers on my desk, trying to look relaxed, casual, and in control. This eventually produces the desired effect. Mary Rohry yells, "Hey, everybody, he's waiting." A couple kids near Mary hear her warning and look over at me. They catch on. One yells, "Shut up, you guys!" A couple more catch on. This cycle repeats until most of the class is attentive, at which point I say again, "As soon as everybody can be quiet for ten seconds, I'll let you all go."

Isolated conversations are still underway. Finally, Mollie McNulty addresses the four or five people still talking. "Listen, you guys, maybe you don't care about missing your bus, but I care about missing mine."

Jack Bixby answers, "I walk." Laughter erupts.

I remind them, "I can't start counting until everyone's quiet."

Silence for maybe three seconds. Laurence Pinkerton in the second row gets a case of the giggles. Kim, row one, turns around and says, "Come on, Laurence, you're gonna spoil it for everyone."

Alice Hanscomb shrugs. "You know, Kim, you just spoiled it, yourself . . . by talking to Laurence."

Kim answers, "Yeah, and you just talked just now."

Alice says, "Yeah and you just talked just now."

Kim: "So did you."

Alice: "So did you."

Kim: "So did you."

Finally, Ryan Peabody, silent until now, stands up. "Okay, I want everybody to shut up for ten seconds, starting now!"

This male bravado is too much for Jack Bixby, who says, "You're cool, Ryan." Ryan stands resolute.

Andy Thornton says, "Your fly's down, Ryan." Ryan moves his eyes down, then catches himself. It's enough to get a few chuckles. Ryan sits.

Nobody says anything. Five seconds. Close enough. I give the homework assignment. Class dismissed.

Thus is played Silence Is Golden, which is not unlike the business of school reform, which goes like this.

Teachers: We want to change but the administration won't go for it.

Administrators: We want change but teacher attitudes are too entrenched, and we have the board to contend with.

Board members: We want change but our hands are tied by the unions and state regs.

Parents: We want change, but the board is unresponsive and the teachers inaccessible.

For schools to change in this country will require an unprecedented exertion of collective (and cooperative) will power. I wonder if that can happen.

"So did we all just waste the last five days?" I asked.

Bill answered. "I don't see it as a waste by any means. I

do think there's a chance for change, but it can only happen very slowly and in small steps. The problem is that the room in which we have to maneuver is so small. It's like the powers that be say, okay, you can design alternative programs as long as you don't stray from the state syllabus and as long as you provide X hours of instruction and as long as you use these tests and this remediation program and as long as you follow these regulations for discipline and as long as you cover these subjects and as long as each kid gets so many Carnegie units and on and on. By the time you get to the end of the list, you've stricken almost every area of serious innovation. All you can really do is tamper with the periphery. The heart of the system is protected."

"So how do you bring about change?" asked Mary.

"By doing what you can on the periphery and at the same time using the political process to lobby hard for getting those core factors altered."

"I say blow the fucking system out of the water," said Jerry. This got everyone's attention.

"Atta boy, Jerry," said George.

"No, I'm serious. Bill is absolutely right. Any effort at reform is just tampering at the edges. You'll still have the same basic system. What you need is to dismantle the system. I mean, if you want real change."

"One well-placed bomb in every school in North America," said Ellie Grosshartig. "I love it."

"That would dismantle the buildings, but I don't think it would change the system," said Jerry. "You'd just see the same damn schools sprout up again, like mushrooms from cowshit."

"So what do you do?" asked Ellie.

"You change the basic economic relationships."

"You give everybody a million dollars," George offered. "What a great idea."

"Maybe not a million," answered Jerry seriously, "but a little ticket each year worth about six or seven thousand dollars, whatever it costs to educate a kid in this country for one year. Anyway, you hand out these tickets to parents, one ticket for every kid they have and you say send your kid to any accredited school you want.''

"Vouchers," said Bill. "We've heard it before. You'd see public schools wither and private schools thrive."

"Yes, but the private schools would no longer really be private since their money would come from government-sponsored vouchers."

Bill said, "I think you'd see schools become very segregated and a huge gap between the quality of schools."

"How is that different from what we have now?" said Jerry. "Talk about mushrooms in cowshit . . . I think you'd see a hundred flowers blossom. Think about it. Let's suppose there's a bunch of tired old teachers like us who decide to hell with the system. They could go out and start their own school and if they can convince enough parents that their school is good then they get the bucks. And they wouldn't just have to go to rich parents. Innovators would not be stuck designing alternative schools for rich kids. You could go into the inner city and get the same money setting up a school there as in suburbia. Individual schools would take on a distinct character and become known for a certain philosophy or approach. Parents would love it because they'd have a choice."

"Would teachers go for it?" Mary asked.

"Teachers who are competent would."

"The unions would never go for it," said Bill.

"That's right," said Jerry. "It would blow collective bargaining out of the water."

"So, Mr. Chief Negotiator, how come you're so hot on the idea?" said Bill, figuring he had Jerry now.

"Because if you're talking about giving more power to teachers, this kind of a plan gives teachers the power in terms of resources to start their own schools, to really exercise their own beliefs about education and say to hell with the system as we know it. That's power. Yes, it would destroy collective bargaining. But remember, collective bargaining came into existence as the only way of empowering a group of workers who individually were powerless because they had no access to capital. So they wielded the only clout they could, the threat of withholding their labor. If you've got a system like I'm suggesting, individual teachers or small groups of teachers are empowered by virtue of the tuition tickets they can get for every student they teach."

I said, "This is like, free enterprise comes to education. Schools compete for students like companies compete for customers."

"Yeah," said Jerry. "Except that it is government sponsored. Every consumer out there, if you want to call them consumers, gets an equal amount of money with which to buy the product. So we preserve the idea of equality of opportunity. What could be more democratic?"

We hashed through Jerry's idea and agreed that if the revolution did not come within ten years, we would all lobby for his plan and then start our own school together. All except for Bob, who said he'd be retired by then, so we all further agreed that Bob would be hired on as a consultant with grant monies that our great little experimental school would no doubt be successful in obtaining.

The idea of tuition vouchers slowly built momentum during the 1980s and at the end of the decade seemed suddenly to be at the center of school-reform debate under the general rubric of "choice." It seemed odd for Jerry Rubicon, our socialist chief negotiator for the teachers' union, to be singing the praises of an idea championed by Ronald Reagan. But then, more than just conservatives were talking favorably about voucher schemes by the end of the 1980s. In June 1990 the centrist (some might say liberal) Brookings Institute released a report by Terry Moe and John Chubb arguing in favor of tuition vouchers. In *Politics, Markets, and America's Schools,* Moe and Chubb suggest that the present economic and political organization of public education renders the system incapable of change.[3] Past reform efforts, they point out, have sought to change practice without addressing the institutional context of schools, that is, the way schools are funded and governed. Practice, they say, is determined largely by funding and governance, and therefore if practice is to

change, funding and governance must change first. Myron
Lieberman argued similarly in *Privatization and Educational
Choice,* published a year earlier, but failed to create a stir,
probably because Lieberman is a known conservative and his
book was not published by a "liberal" think tank.[3]

By 1990, the choice issue had shaped up into two different concepts: one that would include private schools and
one that would be limited to public schools. Under the first
scheme, parents receive from the government a voucher, in
the form of a document or stated policy, for each school-age
child. This voucher may be submitted to *any* school, public
or private, where the parent chooses to enroll the child. The
school then redeems the voucher with the state for the cost of
tuition. Under a public school choice plan, parents select
from among *public* schools within a geographic area. The
main difference between the two is that one allows the possibility of public school money going to support traditionally
private (possibly sectarian) schools while the other keeps public education within the realm of traditional public schools.
We will return to choice later. These are compelling ideas
that are slowly (in some cases not so slowly) finding their
way into mainstream thinking and practice.

Our week was up. Bill said the report would be turned
in to Dr. McBrave by the end of the month and George invited
us all over to his place for a beer to celebrate the coming of
the revolution.

So what did our model high school look like? Essentially, we took the one thousand kids and eighty educators at
Amesley and we broke them into groups of about one hundred kids and eight educators each. The support staff was
redistributed in such a way that each group got a full-time
secretary and a full-time teacher's aide. Each group stayed
intact for six years, starting with the kids in grade seven and
staying with them through graduation. The way we designed
it, each team of educators was given maximum freedom to
design the programs they thought best suited their group of
kids. Kids would be randomly assigned. We included a list of
competencies that we felt every Amesley graduate should pos-

sess. This was the extent of the syllabus, as it were. Teaching teams were free to use whatever means to reach those goals.

We realized we were making some sacrifices in so designing the school. Kids would be limited in the range of electives they could take, and teachers would lose the luxury of isolation; they would have to learn to be part of a team. But we felt the advantages outweighed the disadvantages. Because of the smaller, integrated groups, true community could flourish; both kids and teachers would feel truly an important part of something, a feeling that would translate into higher motivation all the way around. And, though the range of course offerings might not be as broad, students could study subjects in greater depth. The idea of individualizing instruction would be much more a reality. And the curriculum and schedule would be flexible since changing them would involve fewer people and fewer levels of bureaucracy.

In order for our plan to work, we recognized that certain obstacles (substantial ones) would have to be knocked down. First, educators would have to accept a role as generalist, capable of being combination instructor/counselor/manager, a role that runs counter to the unfortunate trend toward ever narrower specialization. Also, the curriculum as set forth by the state education department would have to be thrown out the window, to be replaced by a streamlined list of broad objectives. It would be the death of standardization and, we agreed, the beginning of higher standards. Finally, community expectations would have to be altered. Parents would have to accept an end to standardization, and they would have to accept that one team might do things differently from the one their son or daughter was on, but that both groups were working toward the same broad goals. Furthermore, the community would have to accept the loss of a varied elective program, a point of pride to most suburban high schools, for the sake of depth.

Over at George's, Jerry Rubicon, loose from a couple of beers, declared it all a great plan that would never work and couldn't we move up the timetable for his voucher scheme.

3.

If You Stand Up, You Will Get Shot

O. J. Dave thought it was a great report. He said it just might herald the beginning of great changes at Amesley Central School District and we ought to print up a copy for every teacher in the district and have meetings and seminars to discuss it. So the report was copied and distributed and meetings were tentatively scheduled and some people read the report and some most likely did not and the meetings never occurred because more "urgent" matters pressed in. Everyone who read it said it was a fine report and it was then tossed to the top of the stack of all the other fine reports and it did little to change anything because after all reports generally do not change people. And, some of us concluded, actions speak louder than words. So a small group of the faithful few began holding monthly meetings to consider what we might do in the short term, that is this year or next, to usher in the New Age.

Meanwhile, though we did not know it then, a year of great upheaval was brewing, what with a new principal (Roberta Walters arrived in September) and the prolonged contract negotiations that were to dominate school life from about December to March.

Actually, all of that is fairly depressing, so I'll tell a story instead.

It was a Thursday afternoon in September. Students were drifting in to Mr. Nehring's room for Le Club, a regular after-school feature for students who do not turn in assignments. Especially on this sunny fall day, faces were considerably glum while I with no show of pity wrote their names in my book. Ruth and Melissa, two generally conscientious students, moped through the doorway with the rest. Their essays on Pakistan, due Tuesday, still had not found their way to my desk.

"Mr. Nehring," said Ruth, who with Melissa still with mopey looks had shuffled to my desk, "do we have to show up today?"

"Isn't that a moot question?"

"Huh?"

"I mean you already showed up. So why are you asking me if you have to show up?"

"You know what we mean."

"Well, I guess you mean do you have to stay. No, you don't have to stay. But if you don't stay, I send a note home and the note says you didn't stay and you didn't do your homework."

"But we showed up," said Melissa, bursting into giggles in a way only ninth-graders can. "But I guess that's moot."

"Next question," I said.

"Well, we have a reasonable excuse for not staying," said Ruth.

"Okay," I answered. "I'm a reasonable person. What's your reasonable reason?"

"We need time to practice the duet," said Ruth.

"The duet," I said.

"Yeah," said Melissa. "See, we take piano and we have a recital and it's for two pianos, you know, a duet."

"Oh, really? What are you playing?"

"The piano."

"No, I mean what—"

"Oh, Schubert Fantasie, Opus 103, Four Hands," said Melissa, pleased.

"My goodness," I said truly impressed. "Who's your teacher?"

"Mrs. Heathwood," said Ruth.

"She comes to our homes," said Melissa.

"Mine, too," said Ruth.

"So-o-o-o, can we be excused?" they said together.

"Absolutely not."

"Ohhhh, Mis-ter Neh-ring!"

"It would be unfair to everyone who turned in their assignments on time. Now have a seat and get your work done so you don't have to come in tomorrow.

"Harumph!" They moved to the back of the room.

Fifteen minutes passed. I got up from my seat.

"I have to run an errand," I said to the handful of students scattered around the room. "I'll be back in a minute."

"Take your time, Mr. Nehring," said Ruth.

"And of course," I continued, "everyone will still be here when I come back. Right, Ruth?"

"Absolutely, Mr. Nehring."

So I left, took care of business, and was back a few minutes later. I decided to take a stroll around the room. Scott was filling in a map of South Asia. Angie was reading— at least, her textbook was open. Jason and Todd were writing a skit for their oral presentation. And Ruth and Melissa were playing the piano.

Wait a minute.

In my absence, their creative little minds had schemed to subvert me. On each of their desks lay three sheets of notebook paper taped together end to end. Across the paper they had drawn several octaves of piano keys. Fingers skipped blithely over the keyboards.

I drew near, saying nothing. Ruth said, "Listen, Mr. Nehring." And with that, they began to sing, each girl her own sort of melody line while fingers danced in a makeshift recital of Schubert's Fantasie, Opus 103, Four Hands. They managed a few full bars before Ruth glanced at Melissa and a wellspring of giggles bubbled to the surface. Hee-hee-hee-hee-haa-haa-haa-haa. Awash with laughter, their performance came undone.

They'd won my heart, and I applauded. "You must be very good pianists," I said.

"Oh we are," said Melissa. "But that's hee-hee-hee-hee moot, right? Haa-haa-haa-haa. . . ."

*   *   *

"I'm sorry, Jim, but this thing is really pie in the sky." Joe Grossi ran into me at the bank of mailboxes in the faculty lounge one morning late in September. Our PAE report was in his hands. He was routing it on to the next person in the math department. Seems O. J. Dave had run short on either funds or enthusiasm and our report, which was to be copied for each and every teacher in the district, materialized only in a quantity large enough to be routed through departments.

"I'm just trying to get the number of kids in my Math 10 class down from thirty," said Joe, "and you're talking about a hundred kids for six teachers? Dream on."

What could I say? I didn't want to proselytize. Joe had been teaching for over twenty-five years. It would not serve the cause to tell him he just needed to have vision, to see the possibilities. There was, no doubt, a time when he had had vision, when he'd seen possibilities, but the cumulative effect of do-nothing committees, administrative mandates, and the relentless parade of classes and kids had clouded that vision and stacked the odds against the possible in favor of the status quo.

Humor. That would be the way to answer Joe. But no clever phrase came to mind.

"I hear you, Joe. It's a pretty messed-up system."

"You're tellin' me," he muttered.

Innovation is a tricky process. It's not really a process,

even, which is why it's tricky. You want change, but you don't want to alienate the people you work with. And if it's real change, that is, change that is systemic in nature, then what you really must change are people's attitudes and expectations, the driving force behind the system. If you restructure the system without restructuring people's attitudes, wait a little while and you'll see the same old system reassert itself. That's why changes imposed from the top fail. They offer mechanical reorganization while failing to address deeply rooted assumptions. That's why the open-school movement of the 1970s failed. We built all these open classrooms, thus restructuring our learning environments, but we did not make any effort to restructure the way we thought about teaching and learning. So when we tried to carry on our weary school practices in a context ill suited, we got chaos.

Case in point.

A friend of mine teaches in a different state. Glenn likes kids and is an excellent teacher. Has been for twenty-seven years. As Glenn tells it, about five years into his teaching career, the district decided to build a new middle school. The architect, together with the forward-thinking superintendent, agreed that a significant body of research was emerging in favor of the open-classroom format. They convinced the board of education. A bond issue went before the voters. The voters approved. It got built. They filled it up with kids and teachers and waited for the revolution.

They got a revolution, but not the one indicated by the body of research. The teachers were never for the idea to begin with. They knew that given an eight-period day and 150 kids and subjects and all the rest, what you needed were classrooms where you close the door and do your thing. Unless you were going to also tear down the curriculum, you couldn't go and tear down the walls.

It was chaos right from the start, says Glenn. Kids shooting paper airplanes from one "class" to the next, constant background noise from the other classes that made it impossible to teach, and generally a continual battle with all the distractions available to students in such an environment. At first, teachers dealt with the distractions by huddling all their students' desks a little closer in a tight circle facing the teacher. But that didn't work because the closeness bred new distractions.

Then, one day, one of the teachers pushed a cabinet across the floor between his kids and the neighbor's kids. They couldn't see each other. A major distraction was blotted out. The idea spread like wildfire in August. Pretty soon makeshift walls were going up all over the place: cabinets, bookshelves, empty boxes, audiovisual equipment, textbooks, bedsheets. A kind of floor plan emerged: squarish classrooms with "doors" opening into a central foyer.

The following September, more permanent "walls" appeared. Seems a number of teachers had the same idea separately and had requisitioned soundproof room dividers over the summer. They were the envy of the school. Next, the teachers' association got involved, and with some notable tact suggested to the superintendent that the open classroom was a wonderful idea that just needed some small modifications like retractable floor-to-ceiling walls between all the classes. That way the teacher could move the walls in place for those few times that they need privacy with their classes. The superintendent, who this time did not cite any significant body of research, agreed. Within three years, the system had fully reasserted itself.

Meanwhile, our PAE report was dying a swift and anonymous death as copies got checked off and routed through departments with customary haste. Just more words along the departmental pipeline of words. Blah, blah, blah . . .

I ran into Bill Pierce in the parking lot one day in October.

"What do you hear about *Blueprint for the Future*?" I asked. The PAE report did have a real name.

Bill said nothing, just looked at me. Then, "That's what I've heard. Zip. Nada. Nothing. No, I take that back. The English department is calling it *Lost Horizons*.

For all their imagination, school reformers are at a loss to tell us how to get from the schools we have to the schools they envision for us. And there's the rub. Maybe because we are a product-oriented culture, we tend to neglect process. Whatever the reason, there is certainly a dearth of good thinking about the *process* of changing schools. How do you get the ball rolling? How do you build interest? How do you build consensus? How do you persuade the opposition? How do you cut through red tape? Where do you get the money? How do you change attitudes? And how do you do all this in an ethical way? These are the questions that chiefly concern somebody trying to make real change in a real school. The questions are not educational in nature. They are political. Maybe *that* is why educationists have neglected them.

*   *   *

Days passed and it became apparent that the English department's penchant for satire was the most attention our report was going to find. I was beginning to wonder in precisely which circumstances it is that the pen is mightier than the sword.

For every aphorism there is an equal and opposite aphorism. To wit, actions speak louder than words.

It was in this spirit that Jerry, Bill, Ellie, and I began meeting on Thursday afternoons in Jerry's room. Our first meeting was never called, it just happened one day after school in November. Jerry's door was open. I stopped by to say hi. We started talking. Jerry was all for revising his five-year countdown for vouchers to one year. He noted the almost total absence of talk about the PAE report, which he saw as confirming his view that schools would never change by the mere exertion of will power. What was needed, he said, was a whole new economic ordering. "Remember," said Jerry, "at base is the economic relationship. If you want to change the system, you change the basic economic relationships of the players. Just give parents those little seven-thousand-dollar tickets and you'll see a hundred flowers blossom."

I was beginning to suspect Jerry was right, but I had to give the system one more try. After all, cynicism must be cultivated. Fair is fair.

Then Ellie happened by. "You guys plotting a revolution?"

"Retrenching," said Jerry. "Our opening salvo was a dud."

"You know, I was thinking," said Ellie. "Maybe this whole thing has been just a little too high profile. Maybe it's better just to quietly work behind the scenes, make some quiet changes and slowly build from there. I mean, instead of trying to win everybody over, you just get together with the people who already agree and try to put something together on your own."

"A pilot program," I said.

"I wouldn't be opposed to the idea," said Ellie.

"I heard that," said Bill Pierce, walking into the room.

"You're drafted," said Ellie.

With this foolish and accidental encounter, our Thursday Afternoon Luncheon Club began. It was a classic revolution, all consensus and no program. It began as common spirit, broke to the surface as undefined chutzpah, and gathered force and direction as it went. Which is to say that though it wasn't planned, it didn't just happen either. All of us, despite the chance occurrence of our meeting that afternoon, were growing frustrated with the status quo. We knew each other well enough to recognize some basic agreement. And we all wanted to move ahead despite the failure of the PAE report. Jerry's open door provided only the opportunity for an event that was bound to happen somehow.

And we needed this lighthearted, consensus-oriented group. The school year, like Wallace Stevens's pigeons, was descending downward to darkness. The faculty was in upheaval over changes being wrought by Roberta Walters (the war over where to hold faculty meetings was heating up), and the imminence of contract talks coupled with a generally pessimistic outlook was filling people's heads with visions of work-to-rule and picket lines. The fact that days were getting shorter as we all tumbled into December didn't help.

And as the faculty grew more legalistic, so did the kids. One day I gave Dick Flooby detention. Dick had been late to homeroom three times without an excuse. He was a high school junior and should be able to get somewhere on time, I reasoned. So, as was my policy, on the third unexcused absence, I pulled out a detention slip, filled it out, signed it, and gave the student copy to Dick. Dick was not phased.

"I'm sorry, Mr. Nehring, but you can't do this," said Dick, less like a complaining school kid and more like an attorney reminding me of my responsibilities.

"I beg your pardon," I said.

"Well," Dick said, "let me begin by asking why I am getting this detention notice." Dick had real prosecutorial potential.

"Because you were late to homeroom three times without an excuse." Anticipating his next question, I continued, "The dates were December third, fifth, and sixteenth."

"And did you inform my parents?"

"Did I inform your parents? Give me a break. Look, Dick, you were late to homeroom, you get detention. Case closed."

"I'm afraid it's not so simple, Mr. Nehring." I had to admire his style. "According to the student handbook, the first disciplinary action is home contact, not assigning detention. Unless you've already called my parents, I don't think you can assign me detention."

"Well, Dick," I said. "Whadaya say we make this the test case. Run it through the system and see what happens." I handed him the slip.

"Okay, have it your way," said Dick.

Sure enough, the following morning I received a note from the office of Assistant Principal George Handelman stating that the first level of disciplinary action must be home contact by the teacher.

"Hello, Mrs. Flooby?"

"Yes, speaking."

"Jim Nehring from Amesley High."

"Yes, Mr. Nehring."

"Your son Richard has been arriving late to homeroom with some regularity. He's supposed to be here by seven forty-five. I thought you should be aware."

"Yes, Dick mentioned you might be calling. He says the traffic is just horrendous downtown at that time of the morning. I'll speak to him, Mr. Nehring."

Next day.

"Oh, Dick."

"Yes, Mr. Nehring."

I handed him the slip. "I called home."

"But I haven't been late three times," said Dick with a concerned look. Then, as if patiently explaining the law to a layman, "Detention is assigned following the third occurrence of a tardy after home contact."

Turns out Dick was right on this one too. Mr. Nehring eventually got the satisfaction of assigning detention to Richard Flooby but only after Richard Flooby got the satisfaction of taking Mr. Nehring for a procedural ride.

As the kids grew increasingly legalistic, so did the teachers.

"That's not the way it works in the real world, you know." This was Joe Grossi complaining in the faculty lounge over coffee one morning. "I mean, we give these kids not only a second chance, or a third chance, we just keep on giving in. So they go away with the feeling that there are no consequences for their actions. The real world just does not work that way. If you don't show up for work one day, you're fired. That's it. Punishments for infractions should be automatic."

This is an attitude held by a certain percentage (not small) of the teacher population: holding kids to a kind of standard reminiscent of worker conditions in the days of the robber barons. It is referred to as the "real world."

Let's see.

One lean summer, I was short on cash; my electric bill lapsed three months before a final disconnect notice arrived. My *Popular Life* subscription runs out in September each year and by June I begin receiving promotional mail to get me to resubscribe. The tone of this mail turns increasingly urgent until, about one month after the subscription has already lapsed, I get a pseudopersonal letter from the publisher telling me what an outstanding opportunity I'm missing and how he, the publisher, because he so values my patronage is offering me a special publisher's discount. This is the real world I know.

The list goes on. How about due process and the court of appeals. Student loans and the IRS. How about tenured faculty and incompetent school administrators. Sorry, I'm hitting below the belt. But somebody's got to say it. Unless a tenured public school teacher is clearly a felon, it is almost impossible to be fired. Seems the union makes regular use of the established grievance procedure, too, and more than one grievance in recent memory has been based on purely procedural grounds. This, too, is the real world.

We digress.

The Thursday Afternoon Luncheon Club met as planned the following week. And Ellie brought a guest speaker: Janet Pauley. Ellie wanted Janet to fill us all in on the history of the gifted and talented program, something she had started at Amesley about fifteen years earlier, which had risen to greatness and over the course of about the last seven years had made a long slow slide to programmatic oblivion. Ellie said if we were going to pilot a new program at Amesley, it would be important to avoid the mistakes of the past. Janet was happy to address us since she relished the chance to vent her bitterness about the fall of gifted and talented. Of course, we still had no clear idea what our pilot program would be, but we knew we wanted to try something, and bringing in Janet as our guest speaker was as good a way as any of avoiding our main task.

"Well, gifted and talented began the year before Eric Lawrence arrived (erstwhile principal of Amesley High). Joe DePaulo—some of you might remember Joe—and I had this idea. It was before gifted and talented had become a regular thing in most districts and we felt it was a worthy idea. We just felt there were a number of really top-level kids who were not being challenged. So we wrote up a proposal to pull all those talented and gifted students out and make a separate program. Joe really was the driving force. I was just the first to say yes when he asked if anybody was interested."

"Who did you give your proposal to?" asked Jerry.

"The superintendent, Dr. Biemer," said Janet. "Remember him?"

"Unfortunately," said Jerry.

"That turned out to be part of the problem, actually," said Janet. "Biemer thought it was good and gave us money and basically indicated to Ed McDonald, who was then in his last year as principal, that he should give us a long leash. I think Biemer wanted to take credit for it basically, and wanted to see it succeed. Then Biemer left. So, after our first year, even though we'd gotten the approval to go ahead, the person who was backing us wasn't around any more. Nonetheless, the program did well that year. All the teachers in the program had smaller class loads and common planning time."

"How did the rest of the faculty feel about that?" I asked.

"You mean fewer kids? It wasn't a problem. I suppose some thought it was elitist. Anyway, we cruised through the first year and I think McDonald started to show a modicum of interest. I mean, he'd be an idiot not to. The program was succeeding. He talked it up in the community and saw that our budget needs for field trips and books and things were taken care of. Then McDonald retired and Eric Lawrence came on board as our new principal. Remember him? I don't think Lawrence ever really bought the program. For the next three years I'd say the program flourished in spite of him. And then Joe DePaulo retired. Remember, it was Joe's idea to begin with. He'd really been the driving force, and I guess I have to admit when he left I really didn't carry the torch the way he had. I mean, he was always in there fighting, making sure we got our budget and seeing that class size remained small and that all the teachers in the program had common planning time. When he left, all those things started to disappear. It's like the program had never become fully integrated into the system so that it never carried on automatically like other programs do. And because there was so much turnover in administrators, you always had to be reselling the program to a new person. You always had to be in there fighting, pushing against the system and forcing the system to accommodate the program."

Janet went on to describe how over the last four years the program had become more or less dismantled. First, they took away the teachers' common planning time, then class size started to grow, and all along the budget was slowly but surely shrinking. It was no longer really a special program, just a core of honors classes that virtually anybody could get into.

Janet finished with a grandiloquent sigh. "So that's the story. The rise and fall of gifted and talented at Amesley High."

Janet's story is typical of much that is truly innovative in schools. First, it succeeds largely because of the charisma of certain individuals. When those individuals leave, the innovation flounders and eventually comes undone. Second, innovation usually costs extra—sometimes a lot extra, sometimes a little. Nonetheless, it is therefore subject to greater scrutiny ("we're spending extra on this, so it better be extra good") and is quickly raided during slim budget years. Third, it requires extra effort on the part of those involved, and human endurance is finite. The little engine that could can climb only so many tall mountains before it just plain tuckers out. And, fourth, innovation, because it occurs in a particular human context, is always subject to the self-interest of numerous individuals who have such concerns as building a résumé, maintaining an image, safeguarding union gains, appearing to be in control, getting recognition, getting promoted, and so on.

All of which explains why the odds are stacked against innovation in favor of the status quo.

*   *   *

After the meeting, I walked out to the parking lot with Bill. "You know, it seems almost that to get a program installed you just have to outlast your adversaries. I mean, if you just keep pushing and plugging away through all the principals and superintendents, eventually you prevail."

"Yeah, and then you retire," said Bill. "And the system just kind of blobs back to normal like you were never there."

Janet was right. The system never really accepted the program because it was structurally different. So it was only by the constant exertion of great pressure by someone, and I guess that was Joe DePaulo, that the system could be forced back enough to make just a little room for this aberration. The thing is, you've got to change the whole system. And that means not just programs but attitudes and expectations and regulations and mandates and it's all fairly mind-boggling.

There are two ways our system of public education will change: either by an unprecedented exertion of collective will among educators, legislators, and the public; or, as Jerry says, by something draconian, something that changes the basic economics of schooling in this country. Something like Jerry's tuition vouchers.

The Thursday Afternoon Luncheon Club had met four times by mid-December and we were beginning to think we'd better approach the powers that be if we were going to get any kind of a program started. We'd decided that while it would be impossible to put in place the model high school idea as we had designed it over the summer, we might put together a smaller teaching team that would embody some of the model school's principles. If we could get some courses scheduled so they would be offered at the same time of day and then have several sections of those courses in a row, we would create a chunk of time shared exclusively by a group of teachers and a single group of students. In that way we would gain a little bit of the flexibility and control that we had designed into our model high school.

*   *   *

"That, everyone, is essentially the idea," I said. "We think it could be put in place without much difficulty. And we'd like to give it a try next year. Whadaya think?"

Sitting around the table were O. J. Dave, Roberta Walters, H. Fred Latimer (assistant superintendent for curriculum), Bill Pierce, Ellie, Jerry, and myself. I had just presented the idea for our pilot program to the group.

"So," Roberta began, "you want to take three ninth-grade courses—English, social studies, and home economics—all offered at the same time with two sections of each placed back to back." Roberta looked tentative.

"That's right," I said as confidently as I could. I'd been selected as spokesperson, having picked the short coffee stirrer.

"I think it's a marvelous idea," said Roberta (I wondered immediately whether she would have been wiser to check out the reactions of her superiors before speaking up). O. J. Dave smiled politely at Roberta. Fred shifted in his seat and held his fist to his mouth thoughtfully.

"Why should we do this?" Fred asked finally.

"Well, we think it has the potential to better engage kids," I said.

"On what do you base that?" Fred had a way of being direct.

I was about to say the seat of my pants when O. J. Dave saved me. "I would say, Fred, there is a significant body of research that supports the concept." Dave and Fred spoke the same language. "It's certainly in keeping with the work of the PAE committee."

The conversation went on a while longer, but it did not have to. It was clear by that point in the discussion what kind of a hand we'd drawn: two face cards and a deuce. Dave and Roberta were with us. Fred was the skeptic. But it was definitely a good enough hand to stay in the game. O. J. Dave charged Roberta to check out the scheduling feasibility with the high school guidance department, and he told Bill, Ellie, Jerry, and me to write up our proposal formally for submission to his office. Fred, not wanting to be a sourpuss, offered a few encouraging remarks, and we departed.

Then the union called work-to-rule.

I should say Jerry Rubicon, our chief negotiator, called work-to-rule. Negotiations had stalled out. A mediator had been unable to reconcile the two sides, and Jerry, who had been burning the candle at both ends between teaching, negotiating, and helping us plot the revolution, felt it was the best way to go.

"Jerry," said Bill, "this is crazy. I mean I understand, but it's crazy." It was our next Luncheon Club meeting. We had just mutually decided that we should suspend further discussion of our project until the contract dispute was settled. (Under work-to-rule, anything beyond contractually required service is suspended to show the community how much teachers do that's extra.) It was an easy decision really, but nonetheless painful. Just when our little engine was building up a head of steam, we had to hold the whole train in idle. Besides, the camaraderie of our group had become a very important survival mechanism as morale among teachers hit rock bottom, and now we'd have to suspend meetings at the time when we most needed them.

So we went about the business of teaching, through the maelstrom of work-to-rule. It was February, that three-month period between January and March. Not much may be said for February. You can't even say it's short because it really isn't even that. The number of days appearing on the calendar is an optical illusion. There are exactly two good things that may be said for February. Here they are:

Snow and snow days.

Snow has a magical effect on a school burdened by workplace tensions and winter doldrums. Like the appearance of a baby among strangers, it distracts, focuses, draws people together, and generally lightens the mood.

"It's snowing!" cried Ashley Morgenthau. And every head in the room turned toward the window. My fifth-period ninth-graders were into a geography lesson on Africa, doing maps and statistical work in groups around the room. Snow had been predicted earlier in the day, discussion of which had already consumed well more than its share of talk as every possible speculation was presented and fully debated.

"If it snows any time during the day, they send us home early."

"No, it's only if it starts snowing before 11:15, and they predict five inches or more by the end of the day."

"So how come you know so much?"

"My mom works in the administration office."

"I remember when we were in fifth grade, it was already snowing before school started and we were like listening to the radio and we even had a radio at the bus stop and they didn't close school. Remember that?"

"I remember last year when they sent us home early and one of the buses crashed and this kid is suing the school for ten million dollars."

Like that. So when Ashley Morgenthau yelled, "It's snowing!" everyone's sense of anticipation was already well primed. And as everyone turned to look, sure enough, big white flakes thick enough to completely block out our view of the football field were falling at a steep angle to the ground.

"Are they gonna close school, Mr. Nehring?" Paul Marconi turned to me and asked.

How am I supposed to know if "they" will close school? But kids always ask. So I have to say something. I feel like the TV news reporter who has to give a report about something that hasn't happened yet. "The president's press secretary will be entering the room at any moment now to deliver what is expected to be the president's response to allegations that . . ."

I could just say, "I don't know," but that would be like the reporter saying he doesn't know when the anchor asks, "And what do you expect the press secretary will say?" It's boring. Zero speculation value. And it being February and all, and the mood of the building being so glum, here's what I said: "Well, I'm sure they'll let us know over the P.A. as soon as any decision is made." A statement designed to have enough speculation value to keep the kids happy but not so much as to keep them distracted from the lesson. No such luck.

"When will they announce it?"

"I bet they'll say something right at the end of class."

"No, I think they'll wait 'til the end of the day."

"Then what are they gonna announce, stupid? Go home early?"

"Oh yeah."

"I think they'll announce it as soon as somebody makes a decision."

"Who decides, anyway?"

"Dr. McBrave."

"You mean O. J. Dave?"

"What?"

"That's what the teachers call him."

Most of the preceding conversations, or something like them, could no doubt have been heard in every other classroom at Amesley High. And probably in the faculty lounge.

The other good thing about February is snow days. Even when they don't materialize, they're still a good thing. They give everybody something to complain about besides the school principal, or those mean teachers, or that intransigent board of education refusing to approve a very fair and respectable contract. For just this one issue, everyone in the building stands united. Even the crabbiest teacher and troublest troublemaker kid may be seen yukking it up about how stupid it is they didn't close school and how they're gonna have a lawsuit on their hands when a bus crashes, and doesn't anybody have any common sense any more, and Chester High and all the other schools in the area were closed. And so the weather provides a bond crossing all lines and we go about our business of math and English and study hall not as adversaries but like strangers thrown together in a lifeboat adrift in a sea of swirling snow and darkened schools across the county.

But the best is when they really call a snow day. The news comes either by radio or (for teachers) via the telephone chain, assuming all those involved do their part. Two years ago Ethel Port made a formal request to Dr. McBrave that in the event of a snow day, the decision to close schools be made before 6:00 A.M. so that we might all just stay in bed rather than rising, showering, and getting breakfast only to find out we could have slept in. It's too bad Dr. McBrave didn't take the request seriously. It was a wonderful idea. Many have been the mornings when I lay in bed listening to AM radio stations read long lists of school closings earnestly wishing to hear, "Amesley Central Schools, closed today." I've even put the telephone on the toilet seat while I was taking a shower so I could be close by in case the telephone chain should reach out to me.

When the announcement actually comes, it is just incredibly wonderful. Though I've never won a trip on a game show, I imagine that's what it's like. "Congratulations, you have won an all-expense-paid vacation for one . . . from school!" The curtain parts and there's a picture of a sunny kitchen window framing a glistening field of snow with me at the kitchen table, reading the paper with a cup of coffee, watching the snow fall.

I've now said everything good about February. We had two snow days during February and two close calls, which as I've indicated also have value. All together the snow days and the close calls got us through February, which otherwise would have been unendurable.

Eventually, the contract was settled. Jerry was not jubilant, but he seemed basically pleased. The other side as far as I could judge seemed to feel the same way. Which means, I guess, that both gave a little and a real compromise was reached. Work-to-rule has a way of doing that, of getting movement. But it's not without its price in terms of tension and ill will, which does not automatically go away when the contract is settled. Every week of work-to-rule, I would say, translates to maybe three months of healing time as far as personnel relations go.

Collective bargaining in public education is a fact of life in almost every state. And job action by teacher unions is not uncommon. Throughout most of its history, the National Education Association (this country's largest teacher union) eschewed teacher strikes as unprofessional. Then during the 1960s, when the rival American Federation of Teachers began to use striking and the threat of strike as an effective bargaining tool, the NEA was forced to do likewise or lose membership. Because of the increasing willingness of teachers' unions to resort to bold job action (strike, work-to-rule, picketing), collective bargaining became a more significant factor in school politics. From a purely partisan standpoint, as a teacher, collective bargaining has achieved much: vastly improved salaries, fair and established grievance procedures, codification of sabbatical policy, elimination of chaperoning requirements, coaching requirements, cafeteria duty, and other add-ons that districts used to assume as part of the job, improved health benefits, and more. Indirectly, all this translates to better schools since good salaries and working conditions attract and retain good teachers. At the same time, however, collective bargaining has hurt the ethos of schools. Contractual constraints (along with state regs and board policies) make it difficult for a principal to assert real leadership. And the adversarial nature of bargaining works against esprit de corps.

Given the historical circumstances of the teaching profession and the political context of public education, the demand by teachers for collective bargaining has been necessary, but is it the best way to run a school? I think not.

*   *   *

The Thursday Afternoon Luncheon Club met again in the middle of March. It was a jubilant reunion. Jerry told war stories from the bargaining table, including the one about how on the first day O. J. Dave had divulged the total dollar figure the board was willing to work with and then spent the next few months trying to backpedal. That's why Jerry called work-to-rule. He knew it was worth holding out for more because there was more to hold out for.

Eventually, we got down to business, which for us, a very unbusinesslike group, meant that we spent the last ten minutes of our meeting agreeing that we had to get the ball rolling. It was time to check back with Roberta to see if our plan would work with the Guidance Department, gatekeeper of the school master schedule. And if that was feasible, then it would be time to go before the faculty and tell them what we were doing. The plan we were working with involved Bill, Ellie, and me teaching two sections each of our respective subjects—English, home ec, and social studies—to a core group of, say, fifty kids over a three-period block of time, which would give us just a little more flexibility with curriculum, grouping, and scheduling than the current system allowed. Jerry, reeling from two months of hard bargaining, agreed to be just an interested observer during the first year of our pilot program.

So we met with Roberta shortly thereafter and hammered out a specific plan that she said guidance could live with—that's just the way she put it, too. Apparently, guidance was not really thrilled about tampering with the master schedule: the kids for our pilot program would have to be "hand scheduled" and that meant a fair amount of work and they didn't know about this new idea and it sounded like an innovation that might have some problems. No doubt their educator radar was up, detecting "innovation" the way most educators have come to experience it: new-idea-from-them which translates into more-work-for-us. But Roberta was persistent—we're lucky she liked the idea—and after all she was the principal, so guidance agreed and it was worked out and Roberta said fine let's do it.

Basically, the program meant that among the three of us (Bill, Ellie, and me) we had two and a half hours each day (three consecutive periods plus passing time) to teach English, social studies, and home economics to a group of fifty kids. How we grouped the kids and structured time within that framework was up to us.

Now we had to present the plan to the faculty, something none of us wanted to do. Because teachers spend 95 percent of their work lives isolated from other adults as they ply their craft, and doing so under less than ideal conditions, the rare occasions when we assemble serve as a kind of a pressure valve. In the faculty room we vent our rage on a daily basis in an informal way. In faculty meetings we vent our rage on a monthly basis in a more formal manner.

"We'd like to get started," Roberta was saying for the third or fourth time. It was April. The contract settlement was old news. The Little Theatre movement had lost all its passion, and for the most part the faculty had accepted its lot in the cafeteria. The real reason the Little Theatre movement had been so strong was that the Little Theatre was much better suited to dramatic rage venting, what with high visibility, good acoustics, and a very plain, identifiable target seated there on the stage. The cafeteria had none of that. All facts that Roberta was well aware of.

"We'd like to get started here." Most of the faculty was now seated. Joe Grossi was correcting assignments behind a pillar toward the rear of the room. The science department, seated together, was yukking it up over some tale that Mary North was telling. Lil Gilliam was working needlepoint in the front row. Bernice wore an olive green suit.

"Okay, could we get started now. If you'll look at your agenda, you'll see that it is very full. I think there are ten, yes, no, eleven items of business." Dramatic pause. "Eliminate the first five. We're going to make this a quick one today." The group breathed a spontaneous sigh of relief. Roberta knew how to win over a crowd.

We breezed through the first three agenda items. Then came us. Roberta spoke.

"As you all know, the Amesley District was awarded a Professional Access to Excellence grant last year by the state education department. Mr. Pierce and Mr. Nehring, who wrote the grant, worked with others to develop a proposal for a model high school. I'm sure you're all aware of *Blueprint for the Future*." There were several audible groans. "Based on that proposal, a pilot program has been developed for next year. And to describe it for you, here is Mr. Pierce, Mr. Nehring, and Ms. Grosshartig."

Dead silence. If I'd known what lay ahead, I'd say forbidding silence.

Bill, Ellie, and I rose. The day before, we'd managed to find a half hour to sit down and put together a presentation. We even had an overhead transparency. We made our pitch, showed how the program looked on the overhead, asked if there were any questions. There being none, we sat down. Thank you very much. Next item on the agenda.

It seemed too easy. It was.

Next morning early, I was pouring coffee in the faculty lounge. Ethel Port stepped up.

"You know, I feel betrayed," said Ethel.

"Excuse me?" I replied. Had Ethel said "betrayed"?

"I said I feel betrayed."

"What about?"

"About your pilot program."

Uh-oh.

Ethel went on to say that this was the first she'd heard of the program and she'd had no chance to put in her two cents and how come the faculty is always the last to find out about changes in the program. And then she got really fired up and said how we were dupes of the administrators and we had been co-opted and didn't we see the writing on the wall and how could we and this is what's wrong with education. I looked at Ethel and said, "Hmm" and was otherwise speechless and Ethel looked at me and then walked away shaking her head.

I had not expected this. There being a dearth of other options, I exited the room. On my way out, I ran into Grace Haverstraw, who was on her way in.

"Jim," said Grace, grabbing my arm. I braced myself. "*Liked* that presentation yesterday. Sounds like a neat idea. You know, it's about time we tried something new around here."

"Yeah."

"Good luck."

"Thanks."

Turned out the effect of our presentation was magnetic, in the truest sense of the word. It either attracted or repelled.

There was Lane Hall, who criticized us for taking on an added burden without gaining additional compensation from the district and didn't we realize the precedent that set.

There was Mike Metcalf, who said how he admired our ability to work with the system and how it just goes to show when you follow all the steps and inform people as you go and seek approval and work persistently, it pays off and job well done.

There was Jan Finkelstein, who said we were making a big mistake and it would never work because with a big interlocking master schedule we'd never be able to bring together all those kids into those three classes.

And then there was Bernice Fleischmann, who said didn't we know interdisciplinary teaching came from the East Bloc and it was essentially a communist idea and she couldn't believe that right here in her own high school in the United States of America this was going on.

And then there was Jerry Rubicon. Bless you, Jerry, a voice of reason and calm. I tumbled into Jerry's room after my last class at 2:30. Jerry was at his desk. This room had become a kind of home away from home over the last few months, a place where I could commiserate or just have a laugh with some friendly, like-minded people. Now, as a new battle was raging, it became a safe haven. I didn't *decide* to go there. I just went.

"Well, if it isn't Mr. Controversial himself," said Jerry.

"Ugh."

"Seems you guys have really stirred up a hornet's nest."

"I don't get it, Jerry. What have we done to merit this huge reaction?"

"You've tampered with the system."

"But teachers have done things like this before."

"Not really. They've experimented with new ideas maybe but always within the confines of their classrooms. You're making changes that go beyond the classroom and that gets people nervous because then they say, how's that gonna affect me."

"But it's not going to affect anybody."

"I know," Jerry interrupted. "And it probably won't affect anyone, at least not this year. But people think down the road. Whenever a change like this comes along they see it as a sort of foot in the door and think it's going to expand and take over the school."

"I hope it does."

"That you better keep to yourself. Just tell Ethel Port she's going to be team teaching with Bernice Fleischmann in two years and you'll really see the shit hit the fan."

"So what do I do?"

"Reef your sails and ride out the storm. By the way, Ethel Port saw me this morning. She wanted to file a grievance."

"She wanted to file a grievance?"

"I told her she was crazy. Actually, I said she couldn't grieve a member of her own bargaining unit. So then she wanted to file against Roberta Walters and I said what for and she couldn't think of anything."

"Jerry, tell me honestly, do you think there's legitimacy to all this rage?"

"Is there legitimacy? Yes, there's legitimacy, sure, but there's legitimacy to what you're doing, too. I think it's a matter of what you want more to protect, a fossilized system of education or a very fragile but promising idea for reform."

Jerry and I talked further. Mostly, Jerry gave me a pep talk. I was feeling unsure about the whole thing. He laughed when I suggested that maybe the faculty should have voted on it. He said it would be impossible to get this faculty to approve anything if that's how we made decisions. But what about democracy in the workplace and all that I asked, to which Jerry replied that there was a difference between democracy and mob rule.

Bill Pierce tumbled into Jerry's room.

"Nehring," said Bill, "remind me never to do anything with you again."

Bill had been accosted all day by the same cast of characters. He told how Lane Hall had accused him of not standing up for teachers and demanding added compensation for taking on an experimental program, and then how five minutes after that Jill Goodman intimated how he'd made such a nice cozy deal with the district and how he'd have smaller classes and a big budget and wasn't it all just hunky-dory.

Damned if you do and damned if you don't.

Jerry finally said he'd learned long ago that if you stand up, you *will* get shot at, and if you don't get shot at it's probably because you're not saying anything of consequence.

4.

No More Gurus

The week after our faculty presentation, Roberta sent me a brochure announcing the annual convention of the American School Principals Association, to be held in New York on May 15–17, and would Bill, Ellie, and I care to go since the focus of this year's convention was school reform and representatives of all the nation's big reform efforts would be there selling their wares.

Would we care to go. Sometimes, my old school friend Alec, who went into big business, tells me about his conventions—always in far-off cities in big hotels with expensive food, heated pool, sauna, the works. The conversation usually winds up with me telling how I get away now and then, too, and how it usually involves a bumpy yellow school bus ride to a less than spectacular attraction no more than thirty miles away with a busload of happy, boisterous teenagers bent on mischief. We pack lunch.

Now our principal was asking us, a bunch of teachers, to go to a real convention, the kind my friend tells about. Did this mean the school would pay for it? I told Bill right away.

He thought it was great. Ellie was not as excited. She said she had a funeral scheduled that week—her way of saying she didn't want to leave her students for that long—not even the lure of the Hotel Regal could draw her away. She said have fun and take notes.

This all made Bill and me feel incredibly guilty. But not that guilty. Next, Bill and I went to Roberta and asked if this invitation meant that the school would pay our expenses. She said O. J. Dave had agreed to cover the convention costs (actually, she said Dr. McBrave) if we'd take care of transportation.

Deal.

New York City is a few hours by car and we arrived at the Regal late on May 14, having left Amesley right after school—actually not right after. We tarried just long enough to get stuck behind a phalanx of twenty school buses all headed down Hudson Avenue spewing diesel exhaust in our general direction, and since it was a warm spring day we had rolled the windows down so that before we got on the thruway we were already thoroughly nauseated.

Wednesday, May 15, we woke to traffic roaring up from the canyon twenty-one floors below our room at the Hotel Regal. Ate breakfast at the hotel café off the lobby with a table much too small for the bag full of convention literature we'd been given at registration and eventually gave up trying to understand the program schedule. It appeared there was a workshop sponsored by a group called the School-University Partnership at 8:00 A.M. Bill said maybe they could put us in touch with other teachers trying out team teaching. It being now 8:20, we decided to go.

Dr. A. Sampson Wilson-Rallston (according to the program) was addressing a crowd of about two hundred in Harvard Square (Conference Room A would have been fine, but, no, the Regal had Ivy League names for all their meeting places). We took seats in the back row.

"The essential mission of the university is one of service, yet we have largely ignored the communities in which we are situated. While secondary education has been not so quietly going kaput in this country, universities and departments of education, specifically, have been utterly remiss in their bystanding. We have merrily continued to conduct research and train educators without a second thought to the chaos swirling around us.

"USP, University-Schools Partnership, is an effort to right that wrong. Since our inception five years ago, we have grown to include twenty-seven institutions of higher learning, among them four major research universities. And we are providing needed services to the public schools in our communities. Again, I refer you to our prospectus for a complete description, but just briefly let me say, shopping-list fashion: we offer textbook selection assistance for school personnel lacking the correct skills for textbook analysis; we offer advanced instruction in teaching methodology for high school teachers ready to move beyond conventional instruction techniques; we offer services for teaching writing so that high school English teachers in particular may see how best to teach writing to their students. The list goes on . . ."

So did Dr. A. Sampson Wilson-Rallston. Then, lo, it was time for questions and answers.

From the front row: "Do you find that teachers are sometimes reticent about receiving your help, as a point of pride, say?"

"Sometimes, yes. And that's unfortunate because we have so much to offer. By and large, though, I think teachers and school districts see that they stand to benefit substantially from our assistance."

From the middle of the room: "In what ways do you attempt to bridge the gulf between theory and practice? I mean the rift between educational research and the utter ignorance that teachers show of it."

Dr. A. Sampson Wilson-Rallston chuckled. "Yes, you're quite right. You've put your finger on a key issue there. As much as we try to get teachers to read the research, they just don't do it. One of our member universities is talking about putting together a research journal that would be geared to teachers—you know, less sophisticated language, more graphics—just to get teachers into the research. But you're right, that's a huge problem."

Bill leaned toward me and said in a voice louder than a whisper that this lady made him want to puke and could we go now.

One persistent recommendation from the literature of school reform in the 1980s was that universities, particularly departments of education, need to become partners with schools. A fine idea, portending much mutual benefit. In reality, however, partnership efforts that I have witnessed have been anything but mutually beneficial. In 1988, Boston University formed a partnership with nearby Chelsea School District.[1] Chelsea was in trouble. It suffered from all the usual ills of urban poverty: low achievement, crime, low staff morale, inadequate resources, racial tension, drugs, the whole lot. What B.U. proposed, and got, was essentially carte blanche to reorganize the schools in exchange for money and "expert" management. This was not a partnership. It was a hostile takeover. And it will fail to the extent that it denies control to local personnel and the community.

More typical than the Chelsea scandal, however, is the simple lack of effort by universities and schools to reach out to each other. Part of the problem is money. University departments of education are usually underfunded. Many universities see their education department as a kind of liability, perhaps a reminder to the public of the university's normal school origins. For a state university struggling to become a university of note, a visible department of education is simply bad public relations. Another problem is that for many departments of education, teacher training and the fostering of good public schools are not top priorities. Research *about* teachers and *about* schools is. This lamentable fact has been particularly well documented by John Goodlad in *Teachers for Our Nation's Schools*.[2] Goodlad, who was himself dean of education at UCLA for fifteen years, shows how departments of education have been sucked into the value system of higher education, which rewards research and tacitly discourages teaching and community service. For arts and sciences, this is unfortunate. For a department of education it is reprehensible. Teacher training and a commitment to work with area schools should be top priority for a department of education and a high priority for the university as a whole.

At the same time, school districts typically make little effort in reaching out to area universities. Again, money is an issue, but pride also is a factor. School-level educators have been viewed (and view themselves) as poor cousins to their counterparts in higher education. Reaching out to the nearby university might be seen as a sign of weakness. And given attitudes in higher education anything close to that of A. Sampson Wilson-Rallston (only slightly overdrawn here), it's easy to see why.

The door had barely swooshed shut when Bill launched in. "My god, I have never heard such condescending horseshit in my entire life. I cannot believe it. I cannot believe it. I mean, am I right?" We started down the hallway.

I said how I liked the part about the magazine on the fourth-grade reading level with lots of pictures and how maybe we should subscribe early.

"Eat shit," is all Bill said.

"Excuse me," said a voice behind us. We turned. "Excuse me, but I noticed I think you had the same reaction to the presentation as I."

"You looking for an air-sick bag?" Bill offered.

Refusing to be put off by Bill's inimitable lack of geniality, the stranger continued to pursue conversation, and we ended up going together for coffee. Most workshops would be breaking soon and we could beat the crowd to the hotel lobby, which was to be set up for the morning break. We sat at the same sort of undersized café table but chose wisely this time not to sort through convention literature. Andy Klingo, our new companion, was an assistant professor of education from the Midwest.

"Ultimately, that organization will fail," Klingo was saying. "I don't see how you can continue to have that sort of one-sided partnership and expect teachers to keep coming back. The essential paradigm is a construct that will not effectuate change."

"What pisses me off," said Bill, "is the arrogance, the presumption that they, that higher education, has all the authority and knowledge and that we, the bumbling brain-dead teacher drones, have nothing to offer. I mean, say nothing about the fact that we're in there working with kids every day and maybe have some insight into learning and most of those pinheads haven't been inside a classroom in twenty years."

"Yes, and the ultimate reality is that in the final analysis, practitioners are in a position most proximate to articulate a correct analysis."

"Proximate, shit. We're on the goddamned firing line every day."

Bill was wound up and getting more so. I mostly listened. Bill went on about *pissed off* and *pinheads* and *intellectual snobs,* to which Klingo was answering with *construct* and *paradigm* and *effectuate* and was basically doing his damnedest in his own academic sort of way to be sympathetic to Bill who was proceeding from *pinheads* to *fuck-offs.*

So why does higher education generally look upon teachers as brain dead? For the same reason the powerful always look upon the powerless as foolish.

Higher-education view of typical classroom

1. Students in orderly columns and rows	*equals*	Teacher primarily interested in control, not learning
2. Students listen while teacher speaks	*equals*	Teacher using least effective technique (lecture) to engage student interest
3. Students appear passive and bored	*equals*	Teacher is boring
4. Teacher makes errors of fact in lecture	*equals*	Teacher sloppy in preparation, underschooled in subject matter

5. Teacher is clearly making no effort to change ill-conceived practice — *equals* — Teacher is interested only in getting paycheck

6. Kids show no respect for teacher — *equals* — Teacher does not demonstrate intelligence that would win their respect

Conclusion: Because teacher is clearly brain dead, we must encourage further regulation, mandate course content, and design foolproof teaching methods so brain-dead teacher won't screw up more kids.

Schoolteacher *view of typical classroom*

1. Students in columns and rows — *equals* — With 150 students, teacher is pressured by circumstances and school administrator to maintain order

2. Students listen while teacher speaks — *equals* — State education department has mandated course syllabus thick with information, and teacher is under the gun to present it all and prepare students for standardized, rote test of factual knowledge

3. Students appear passive and bored — *equals* — School day is organized as relentless parade of forty-five minute lectures

4. Teacher makes errors of fact in lecture — *equals* — Teacher was asked to teach course out of area of expertise the day before school term began and is working like the dickens to stay ahead of the kids

5. Teacher appears to make no effort to change ill-conceived practice	*equals*	Teacher has no time to reflect on practice in order to reconceive it; teacher knows that he is powerless to change state mandate but nonetheless takes time to work actively in teacher union because he recognizes that the problem is essentially one of power and that collectively through the union, teachers who are individually powerless have some collective clout
6. Kids clearly have little respect for teacher	*equals*	They know he has no real power and that in the system of public education he is low man on the totem pole and that therefore anybody who is a teacher can't be very bright or ambitious

Conclusion: In spite of what cynics may charge, the teacher is an idealist and keeps on doing what he does.

Fact is, teachers and academics talk past each other because their analysis of what's wrong with education is so different. The leisure class telling the oppressed that if they would just bathe and stop being lazy maybe they would amount to something. And the oppressed just saying, "Fuck you."

This does not help matters.

Bill eventually tired of his abusive tirade and Andy Klingo ran out of latinized verbs. Somehow, though, a gulf was momentarily bridged, and both seemed elated about that. We exchanged addresses. Klingo rose to leave, we shook hands, and he left.

Bill and I next headed off for round two of convention

action at Princeton Hall, where we were to learn about the Model for Efficient Instruction, not so much because we thought we'd learn something but because we'd been hearing about M.E.I. from teachers in other schools near Amesley and figured we'd better be informed about the latest fad. The M.E.I. founder himself, Mordecai Potter, in the flesh, would be in Princeton Hall addressing eager hearts.

There was a huge TV screen at the front of the room, which was already packed ten minutes before showtime. We stood at the rear. Against one wall stretched a great banner that read "M.E.I. and You"; under the banner stood a table with empty boxes in which presumably there had been M.E.I. propaganda already ravenously consumed. All around were enthusiastic educators practicing their Gestures.

Promptly at 10:30, a man entered through the rear door, strode purposefully down the center aisle, and placed himself squarely, front and center.

"Good morning, ladies and gentlemen." Instantly, he had the group's attention. "I am not Mordecai Potter." There was a chuckle among the group: they wanted to show the man he didn't have to say that, they knew what Mordecai Potter looked like—these were real M.E.I. aficionados. "My name is Roland R. Robard and I will be representing the M.E.I. team for you this morning. Dr. Potter regrets that he was called away for personal health reasons (here a gasp from the M.E.I.ers who track the aging Potter's health), but he made a videotape especially for this occasion which we will now go to with no further ado."

Roll 'em, Roland.

The tape began with a small, balding, elderly man— the good Doctor Mordecai W. Potter—personally addressing members of the American Principals Association. It then went into an introduction/demonstration of M.E.I. using earnest young teacher models male and female. Dr. Potter appeared mostly as a voice-over during demonstrations.

"The Model for Efficient Instruction rests on the premise that certain body movements, certain gestures of the face, arms, torso, et cetera, are universally recognized to convey certain messages. Through painstaking research conducted over the span of my professional life, I, assisted by an ever-growing M.E.I. team, have deciphered these messages and developed an actual vocabulary of body language for educators. Clearly, this is knowledge of great immediate value to classroom teachers. It is not vague pedagogical theory nor is it impractical, pie-in-the-sky philosophy. It is concrete. It works. And you can use it Monday morning when you walk into the classroom.''

Sounds great, Mordecai. Tell us more.

"What's more, you probably already possess a rudimentary knowledge of this language. Think about the traditional image of the old-fashioned schoolmarm, recalled in the mind's eye by the wagging index finger, the hand on hip, the forward-leaning torso (video shows youthful model unconvincingly made up as schoolmarm assuming stiffly each gesture as Dr. Potter announces it). The tight lips (close-up of tight lips), and the furrowed brow (close-up of quivering brow). This person speaks sternness (camera pull-back to show full view of model) with her whole body." All of this was very comical but the audience was not laughing.

"We now know, as a result of dogged research, that the message conveyed by these gestures does not result, under most circumstances, in efficient instruction. By way of introduction to the M.E.I. approach, we will now show three sample gestures which our research has revealed to be more efficient, that is, more successful in motivating students to want to learn.

"Jonathan here (referring to a new model on the screen) is demonstrating gesture A1A: assertive/concerned (erect posture, left fist on rear quarter hip, right hand, also in fist, to chin, eyes wide, eyebrows raised). This gesture, truly a combination of gestures, has been proven effective in responding to student questions both by increasing the attention span of the student who asks and drawing out further questions from others in the class. (Camera pans to student desks where neatly groomed boys and girls are politely seated. Several raised hands wave to the air.)

"Perhaps you are wondering why we call this gesture A1A (A1A appears in block letters on screen). The first A stands for Assertive. The "1" stands for "concerned," concerned being just one of several assertive gestures. The second A stands for personality type A. Each of us, we have discovered, possesses one of four personality types. Not all gestures are appropriate to all personalities. The assertive/concerned gestures that Jonathan just modeled for us are suited to personality type A. Let's now take a look at two more assertive/concerned gestures, A1B and A1C, and learn more about both the vocabulary of body language and our personality types."

So went the videotape, with Dr. Potter's kouri models performing in all their stony flawlessness while Dr. Potter's soothing voice provided polished, sensible-sounding commentary. The tape lasted exactly forty-five minutes. The man knows his audience.

On went the lights. Roland R. Robard bounced up from his front-row seat and launched into the live portion of today's presentation, the M.E.I. workshop.

"May I see the hands of all the M.E.I. masters in the room?"

M.E.I. masters?

About twenty people raised their hands. "May I see the hands of all the M.E.I. journeypersons?" Maybe thirty or forty hands. "And all the M.E.I. apprentices?" About fifty hands. "The rest of you we shall assume are new initiates."

Bill and I eyed each other warily.

"Very good. For this portion of the program we will conduct a Phase 1 workshop. I'm going to ask all journeypersons to be the small-group leaders and to see if you can locate one to two apprentices as your assistants. The M.E.I. masters, I'd like you to assemble at the front of the room where I will be conducting a Phase 4 Tier 6 demonstration. Let's take a half hour, then reassemble. Any questions? Very well. Begin."

Being neither masters, journeypersons, nor apprentices, nor being especially desirous of entering this modern-day guild system, Bill Pierce and I decided to just wait where we were at the rear of the room by the door, which was not locked. I checked.

As the workshop proceeded, Bill and I found it difficult to maintain our façade of serious, interested observer (we were already no doubt a little suspect for not participating) as small groups of "new initiates" attempted the Gestures under the direction of journeypersons, like a group of overweight American tourists learning tai-chi from Chinese masters. We just managed to keep from bursting out laughing before the door swung closed behind us.

Every year, it seems, there is at least one new fad, one new instructional technique that is advertised as the guarantor of teaching success. In recent years we have seen the Learning Styles fad based on research by Anthony Gregorc; cooperative learning technique, with numerous gurus; the Effective Teaching Model developed at UCLA under the direction of Madeline Hunter; and the dictae of authentic assessment.[3] Typically, each fad begins as a fairly sound body of research but, as it enters the whorl of faddism, becomes mythologized as the Holy Grail of successful instruction. Each gains its following of devotees. There are increasingly heated debates over fine points of interpretation (is this what our founder meant?), and matters of disagreement become issues of orthodoxy and heresy. Somehow, whatever value the idea originally possessed is debased by the education establishment's treatment of it.

Why does this happen? Why does the education establishment seize upon attractive ideas in this perverse way? There are several reasons. First, there is a perpetual feeling in education that whatever we are presently doing does not work, and therefore something different has immediate appeal. Second, ambitious administrators are eager to exploit this sense of inadequacy in order to gain credit as the one who brought in the new _____ (fill in the blank) technique to solve the _____ (fill in the blank) problem. Third, the education establishment has largely bought into the bureaucratic ethic, which dictates that "expert" policy makers (bureaucrats, educationists) develop educational programs, then "technicians" (teachers) implement them recipe fashion in schools. This thinking assumes of course that programs are broadly applicable and that kids are predictable and alike. This view also suggests that successful teaching is really just a matter of applying the right technique. Therefore, find the right technique, train your teachers in its correct application, and you will have a successful school. The fourth and really troubling reason all this happens is that teachers buy into it. The frenetic nature of teaching puts one in such a state that any rope, no matter how frail, dangled down into the abyss will be seized as a chance to get rescued.

The day went on. We attended several more workshops, none of which was especially memorable, had dinner at the hotel, cafeteria style, as part of the convention "economy package" (our fault—O. J. Dave had given us carte blanche, but I had checked the wrong box when I filled out the form). We decided to skip the evening program when Bill saw a poster in the lobby advertising an education film festival. Tonight, a double feature: *Up the Down Staircase* followed by *Don't Shoot the Teacher* (an offbeat Canadian classic, which I recommend to all educators everywhere). Our evening turned out to be the most instructive part of the day. A good dose of reality, even if it was all celluloid and fiction (kind of like Mordecai Potter?). We wound up the evening with coffee and apple pie at an all-night diner across from the theater.

"Do you think business conventions are like this?" asked Bill, who sat across from me in a booth at the front window.

"I can't imagine," I said. "I mean, I can't imagine a whole group of adults standing in a room and practicing their Gestures like that. I'm not even sure that happened today. Did that really happen? Are people really that desperate?"

"You're right," said Bill. "It's desperation."

"You know what educational research is, Bill?"

"A waste of time?"

"Well, that, too." I laughed. "It's the science of codifying the obvious. I mean what absolute diddly, the vocabulary of body language, gesture A1A, assertive/concerned, constipated/aggressive. Did you know, Bill, that every person on this planet falls neatly into one of four personality type categories? Did you know that the five-hundred seventy-three body gestures all mean the same thing to everybody? Did you know that, Bill?"

"Nehring."

"Yes, Bill."

Bill held up his left hand and raised the middle finger obscenely.

"Bill!" I said aghast. "That is not one of the five-hundred and seventy-three official gestures."

"Just call it five-seventy-four."

We got smart for Thursday morning breakfast and brought just one piece of convention literature, our two-page program overview. This morning we had a choice of Assertive Discipline in the Classroom and Hallways, the Heilbrun System of Stress Reduction, and Creative Time Management, none of which sounded worthwhile. We didn't want to hear about how to cope with the system we had, we wanted to hear from people who were changing the system. Then we noticed, on the back of the second sheet, a small announcement for a program of site visitations. It involved a van ride to three different schools around the city that had gained attention for various reasons. There was a ghetto school in Harlem known for a tough, effective principal; an alternative school on Manhattan's Upper West Side that was begun in 1969, had managed to survive the 1970s, and was still thriving; and a large conventional public high school in Queens that had been divided into several schools within one building.[4] This was clearly the thing for us. It gave us a full day away from the insanity of body-language Gestures, teacher bashing, and coping strategies. And it was free. The New York City Schools provided the van.

The yellow van pulled out of the hotel garage into midtown traffic at 8:15, fifteen minutes late. We'd waited for more people, but the van, which had room for nine passengers, was carrying just six. I guess the tidy logic of Mordecai Potter and the coping strategies of a dozen other education gurus had more appeal than a journey into the heart of darkness. And so we bounded uptown, five seekers of truth plus our guide and driver, toward a rendezvous with a school principal who was too busy to attend the annual convention of the American School Principals Association, even though it was just two miles away.

José Moreno, principal of George Washington High School, was a white conservative's dream come true. Born in Puerto Rico, raised in Harlem by an elderly aunt, he managed to survive the public schools, went on to City College, began as a math teacher, and had worked through the ranks to the principalship of George Washington High. The elderly aunt had worked two domestic jobs and refused all assistance programs for herself and José. José believed in discipline, hard work, and not blaming your troubles on Whitey. That's how he ran his school.

We arrived as classes were changing. The exterior of the building was covered with graffiti, but inside the halls were clean and orderly, qualities apparent even through the mayhem of passing time. No Walkmans, no boom boxes, nothing written on the lockers, no yelling. In fact, the kids showed visible restraint as if they knew they'd have to answer to Mr. Moreno if they misbehaved.

We were led to the principal's office by an efficient-looking secretary who took short, quick steps. As we entered, Moreno stood up behind his desk, where he'd been seated. As he did so, the backs of his legs hit the front edge of his desk chair so hard that the chair went skidding across the floor and almost struck the wall a good five feet behind him. That's how much energy the man had. We were introduced and Mr. Moreno (definitely not José) took us at once back out to the halls, gesturing broadly and talking quickly as if he needed to get this tour done fast in order to get back to work—efficient but not rude.

First stop, the boys' room at the end of the hall on the first floor. Moreno led the way into the bathroom and called to the women in our group that the coast was clear. The bathroom consisted of glistening white tile, stalls with doors, an intact mirror over each sink, soap in the soapdish, toilet paper—rolled toilet paper—in each stall. There was not a trace of tobacco smoke. The room smelled of ammonia disinfectant.

"We have rules at George Washington," Mr. Moreno was saying. "Students know these rules. And they know that if they break them, they will be punished. Consequently, they obey the rules. We have clean lavatories."

"We have rules, too," Bill ventured. "But we don't have bathrooms like this."

"It's because you have weak-in-the-knees administrators who are afraid to enforce. Here . . ." Mr. Moreno pulled from his breast pocket—he was wearing a three-piece suit—a tri-folded sheet. "These are the rules of George Washington High School, what every student in this building can and cannot do. On the back is laid out in very clear language for all to see the consequences of breaking those rules, nature of offense and nature of punishment for first offense, second offense, and so on. It's very simple. When I or one of my lieutenants has a disciplinary conference, it is very short. We verify first whether the student indeed committed the offense, and then we assign the punishment according to our disciplinary code."

"Aren't there sometimes extenuating circumstances," asked one of the other members of our group. "I mean, in a place like Harlem . . ."

"With all due respect, ma'am," Moreno launched in, not missing a beat, "my entire life has been an extenuating circumstance. And the same may with all probability be said for seventy-five percent of the student body of George Washington High School. But I did not make it to where I am today by some well-intended but misguided liberal adult claiming extenuating circumstances on my behalf every time I misbehaved. And neither will any of my students succeed through excuses for extenuating circumstances. We are responsible for our actions. We do what we do on our own account, and we therefore must face the consequences. At George Washington High School, you may not blame your misbehavior on your broken home, your absent father, your drug-addicted mother, your building with no heat, the man passed out in the hall, your job after school, or the welfare check that got stolen out of the mailbox. You behave, or you get punished. And that's how you learn. That's how you learn to be a survivor.'' I imagined Moreno giving this speech to every kid sent to his office.

"We will now take a tour of the classrooms." Mr. Moreno turned on his heels and led the way.

Moreno marched up to a classroom door at mid-hall, then stopped short and, assuming a quiet, respectful air, slowly turned the knob and opened the door just enough to usher us through one at a time. Moreno came in last and closed the door behind him. "Miss Philippe, Math 11," he whispered. We lined up along a bulletin board beside the door. Before us was a sea of students, probably thirty-five, all columns and rows, neat and tidy. Miss Philippe stood to our left, at the front of the room, with the students' desks facing her. She was tall, slim, and elegant, with light brown skin and high cheekbones. She looked like Nefertiti. Her whole body seemed to arch back with regal grace. When she looked down at her students, she didn't lean her head forward, she just shifted her gaze down. Her demeanor was commanding, if the slightest bit strained as six strangers lined up at the back of her room.

The lesson proceeded. Miss Philippe asked questions, students raised hands, Miss Philippe snapped her fingers to recognize the student she wanted. Twice she called on students who did not raise their hands. One gave a passable answer, to which Miss Philippe responded, "That's good, André. See, you knew it." The other said he didn't know. Miss Philippe said, "You not doin' your homework 'gain, boy? You know that don't pass muster roun' here." I had a feeling Miss Philippe and Mr. Moreno got along quite well.

Moreno gave an approving nod to Miss Philippe, then led us quietly out the door. We walked likewise into another classroom, a ninth-grade English class. An older white man was lecturing students about the Globe Theatre, seated at his desk. Again, neat columns and rows of attentive students. We exited. Then in the hallway Mr. Moreno said, "Okay, you pick one." We looked at each other. Moreno touched the shoulder of the woman who had brought up extenuating circumstances and said, "You, young lady. Pick a classroom that you would like us to visit."

"Any one?" she asked.

"Your choice," said Mr. Moreno.

She—Patty—thought a moment, then said, "Okay" and led us around the corner to a hallway that we had only passed through earlier. She stopped in front of a door with opaque glass. On the glass, large letters announced Internal Suspension.

Mr. Moreno smiled. "Good choice."

We entered. The room was light and airy, lit by a bank of tall windows against the far wall with venetian blinds that were fully open. Probably a dozen students sat in columns and rows with wide spaces between them. The students visibly stiffened on seeing us, especially Mr. Moreno, enter the room. Mr. Orteaga—his name was written on the blackboard—sat at a desk before the students. All, including Mr. Orteaga, were busy with desk work. Moreno strode over to Orteaga's desk. They whispered back and forth, then Moreno turned around and made a sweeping gesture with his arm, inviting us to circulate around the room, which we did. Mr. Moreno stopped at the desk of a small boy with huge white eyes bulging from his head. Mr. Moreno spoke and the boy looked straight ahead, stiff as a board. "You got your cigarettes today, Joshua?" The boy's lips moved a little, fumbling for the words that would assuage Mr. Moreno's temper, but they didn't come. "Any loose Marlboros in your locker, Joshua? Should we check?" Those right words still would not come. The boy's gaze stayed dead ahead. Mr. Moreno wrapped his big hand around the boy's shoulder and kneaded. "You're a good boy, Joshua. You stay that way." Joshua kept looking ahead.

Nobody said anything for a long time during the bumpy ride back downtown. I suspect we were each trying to sort out the enigma of José Moreno and George Washington High School. Here was a man who believed in firm, consistent discipline and who carried that belief into practice in a tough ghetto school. And it worked. Maybe Mr. Moreno should have been presenting at the Principals Convention. Maybe all we had to do was clone José Moreno for every principalship in every high school in the country. Why not? Why argue with success? On the other hand, while it was clear that José Moreno was a good cop, it was not clear whether he was a good educator. He had certainly created an environment in which students might be found in their seats at the right times and attentively so. But what happened once that was done?

Well, for one thing, you could teach.

Next stop was the Rainbow School on West 83rd Street, a publicly funded alternative school that managed to hold its own with money from participating school districts around the city and a patchwork of grants from government agencies and foundations.

Bill Wittle had been its principal since 1969 when the school began. He had the look of an ex-hippie who'd been mainstreamed with only partial success. His hair went down past his ears and was cut in a way that suggested it used to go down to his waist. He wore round wire-frame glasses and a neatly trimmed beard, again suggesting some earlier version that was more extravagant. His clothing was denim a la Marlboro Man and, when we met him standing in front of a chalkboard during an all-school presentation, he was holding a piece of chalk like it was the brand of cigarette he used to chain smoke.

"Good morning. Please have a seat anywhere. We're just about done," Bill called from the front of the double-sized classroom as he saw a group entering at the rear. We'd been directed by the office secretary (who was a student) to proceed to the Town Meeting. This was the Town Meeting. Bill Wittle presided. Everyone else—teachers, students, custodial people, and any others, about eighty people all told—sat in folding chairs arranged in several curving rows. We sat at the back and watched. Just as we were sitting down, a hand went up in the row ahead of us. A small boy, a freshman I guess (did they call them that?) raised his hand. He was recognized and spoke.

"I mean no disrespect to our visitors, but I object to the presence of noncitizens at a closed Town Meeting." There was a bit of a stir among all present and many eyes shot to the back of the room toward all those strangers. Bill flashed us an awkward smile. He spoke, "I don't know whether we have determined whether this is a closed meeting. Could somebody check the by-laws on this, please?" Around the room a number of people pulled out a booklet and began thumbing. An eager girl near the front, older, maybe seventeen, raised her hand and was recognized.

She said, "According to statute seventy-one-dash-three—it's on page twelve near the top—all Town Meetings will be open to the public. Only by majority vote of the citizens present at the commencement of the meeting may the session be closed."

Bill spoke. "Then I'll rule that the meeting is open—it seems pretty clear—and the visitors may stay." The awkwardness went out of his smile.

He continued. "Okay, now the next matter before the body has to do with the installation of a retractable wall for the all-purpose room, where we are here assembled. Cost is estimated at ninety-three hundred dollars. The work would be done next summer. Jeff Summers feels this is necessary to accommodate the new writing program, which calls for multiple small-group meetings. The only way these can be arranged is through the addition of two new classrooms. Dividing the all-purpose room seems the cheapest alternative. I'd like to ask Jeff to speak on behalf of the proposal first. Jeff."

An older man with mustache and slightly wild, graying hair, tweed jacket, and generally rumpled appearance, rose. "Bill has fairly well outlined the proposal. It's clear why we need the space. The cost is not great, and since I don't anticipate opposition to the idea, I won't prolong our deliberations. Thank you." He sat.

Bill spoke again. "Does anyone care to speak opposed?"

A hand went up immediately from the middle of the crowd and was recognized. A robust white girl and a thin, deeply colored black girl stood up together. The black girl spoke. "We're very concerned that at a time when the scholarship fund for our summer camp program is at an all-time low of eight-hundred twenty-seven dollars, we're sittin' here talkin' about spending ten thousand on some dumb wall."

Jeff Summers interrupted. "Object to the characterization of the partition as dumb. No need to state the obvious."

There was a ripple of laughter. Bill addressed the girl. "There is a request—"

"I know, I know, I heard."

Shortly, Bill made clear to the two girls that right as their cause was, general fund money, which was being used for the partition, could not be mingled with the scholarship fund, which was a special category of the budget. The partition passed by voice vote. A few other matters were discussed and voted on, then the meeting was adjourned. Students, teachers, and support people ambled back to their varied activities around the building.

We had lunch with Bill Wittle in the cafeteria—several folding tables set up in the all-purpose room—and Bill told us all about Rainbow School's democratic ideal, which apparently all took seriously, as evidenced by the fact that students voted on the use of discretionary money granted to the principal each year. The school also had an active, student-run press, which reported not only on school news but the local community as well. What about discipline? Bill said there wasn't too much of a problem, which he attributed to the fact that students had real power and did not feel as strong a need therefore to terrorize the school community. He said rules applied equally to all and major offenses were handled by the school's court, complete with jury. Someone asked if maybe the lack of discipline problems had something to do with the fact that kids were specially chosen for the school. Bill conceded yes, but added that there were no special qualifications for admission besides a desire to attend this sort of school. And, he added, his school represented a broader cross section of socioeconomic backgrounds than most other public schools.

We piled into the van after lunch and headed out to Queens. The enigma of José Moreno and George Washington High School was now further complicated by the fact of Rainbow School. The first was rooted deeply in authoritarianism, the second with roots equally deep in democracy, and both functioned well in their own way.

JFK High School held five thousand students drawn from endless blocks of small, neat rowhouses inhabited by a kind of white-collar proletariat: clerks, secretaries, low-level computer operators—people who spend their hours at work transposing other people's information from one medium to another. JFK had the factory look of a suburban high school, only stripped of its chrome trim and surrounding green space. There was asphalt and dirt and a broad sky that looked like it should always be a mottled gray hanging over the school and those endless blocks of rowhouses.

School had already let out and we met with the principal, Armand Cisnerian, who took us on a tour. The halls had that look typical of schools at this time of day, just after the kids have left and before the custodians swing into action, the look of a baseball park after a game. Small trash was scattered everywhere. Dried mud made a wide strip of grime down each corridor. Armand spoke as we walked the halls. "JFK is a school that's seen it all. You had your student riots in seventy-one, you had your touchy-feely curriculum in the seventies, we had an alternative school for a couple years, then we had your Ronald Reagan back-to-basics in the eighties. They had this principal here then who I swear used to run a boot camp. Kids hated him. Tried to burn his house down, vandalized his car. He finally left, and things just kinda settled into their usual status quo chaos. That's when they put me in as principal. I been here twenty years—taught earth science, then I directed guidance. Anyway, when Jordan left— he's the hard-ass guy—I guess they figured they'd try promoting from within."

Armand Cisnerian, a short, robust, energetic and hairy man—except for the top of his head—pointed out the usual uninteresting school sites as we went: library, classrooms, displays. The tour was standard. Cisnerian's story was not.

"So they hire me and I come on board and see a school that's seen it all, like I said. The kids just seemed to kinda mope along and the staff the same. So I tried to figure out what to do. So we had some meetings and I got this picture from the teachers that they didn't want some new-fangled program—you know, the latest education wizard with all the answers—they just wanted a good solid program. Problem was, nobody agreed on what was a good solid program. We had some teachers who were heavy into discipline and law and order and at the other end of the spectrum were your teachers who were into kids becoming self-directed and a democratic environment and all that.

"So since nobody could agree, I finally came on this idea that we'd just split the school up into five littler schools and each littler school could run itself as it pleases. I already had three assistants, so I convinced the board to hire two more and all five of 'em became deans of our schools.

"Then we had to figure out how to split everyone up. So I decided I'd have each of my assistants give a speech and then the teachers could decide whose school they wanted to be in. Some people said I was crazy, and my assistants bellyached to high heaven, but they did it—you know, 'cause I'm the principal." Cisnerian let out a short burst of laughter and his broad neck, already overflowing a tight collar, turned a deeper red.

We got fairly well into the guts of the building on our tour, when Cisnerian suddenly turned and declared, "Ah hell, you guys know what a goddamned high school looks like. Whadaya say we head back to the office for coffee." No one objected.

Over coffee, Cisnerian explained how his new regime, in place for four years, was producing some interesting results. Each school was developing a kind of personality. One was very strict; another, progressive with an active student government. One, said Cisnerian, was beginning to look like "one of those alternative schools—you know, the kind where kids are always making murals." He said the board was now considering the possibility of letting parents choose which school to send their kids to. "You'd think an idea like that's got a snowball's chance in hell, but by god I thinks it's gonna make it."

Three schools: George Washington High, Rainbow School, and JFK. All different. All successful.

Sort that one out!

Here goes. The success of any one high school does not hinge on the implementation of any instructional model. The teachings of Mordecai Potter or the wisdom of any of a dozen current gurus was not a factor in any of the schools we visited. That much was clear. Beyond that, not much was. In fact, the differences were much more apparent than any commonalities. These schools all differed from each other in size, ethnicity, and class. Each had a distinct ethos: authoritarian, democratic, manifold. Their principals differed in personal style and philosophy. Each had a particular history different from the rest. There was certainly no formula I could generalize from their histories that could replicate success elsewhere. Success, even, would be differently defined in each school, yet there was no denying that in some way each school had achieved a measure of it. The principal did seem to be a factor. Yes, in each school, the principal was a strong or at least enduring personality. But beyond that it was all just muddle and quirkiness. Yet somehow, in each case, consensus emerged—basic agreement among enough people to drive the school toward a certain new reality.

Beyond all the muddle, there is just one factor present in all these schools (and, indeed, in all public schools that are outstandingly successful) that may explain their success. And that is autonomy. As the result of circumstances that in each case are unique, such schools somehow break away from the bureaucratic controls under which public schools labor and win a special dispensation to chart their own course. Rainbow School did it through a good deal of grantsmanship, which provided substantial funding free of the usual regulatory encumbrances. In the case of José Moreno, his school was in such a disastrous state that involved people were willing to take risks and try something different because there was so little to lose. It couldn't get much worse. And in the case of JFK High School, again, frustration with the status quo had reached a level sufficient for the community and the faculty to be willing to experiment with a radical overhaul.

This notion of autonomy is explored in *Politics, Markets, and America's Schools.*[5] Moe and Chubb attempt to identify the factors that make a school successful. Based on a huge nationwide data base, they conclude that there are three: family background, student ability, and school organization. The first two come as no surprise, but the last suggests that success in education is partly under the control of educators and therefore we need not despair that the dice are loaded against disadvantaged kids. There *is* something schools can do to make a difference. What we can do, or rather must do, is find ways of effectively organizing schools.

Moe and Chubb say further that effectively organized schools are characterized by four qualities: a strong principal, a harmonious and professional staff, clear goals endorsed by all, and an orderly environment. These qualities, they say, emerge when schools are given the room to act autonomously, to develop their own best practices free from overregulation. Within public education, however, that is difficult to achieve because of the multiple layers of governance and regulatory constraint. When schools in the public sector achieve autonomy, they argue, it is the exception, rather than the rule. Certainly, the three schools on the tour were exceptional. Their high level of autonomy is unusual. The question is, can this same high degree of autonomy become the norm rather than the exception under the present system of public education, or must we, as Moe and Chubb argue, dismantle the present system with something like a voucher scheme to grant schools the room to become autonomous and effective?

The third and final day of the conference was really a half day, ending in a big luncheon for all in the ballroom. At breakfast, people at the table next to us were practicing Gestures, a sight that greatly affirmed our decision the day before to hit the road. Of the offerings this final morning, none appealed.

Three days in New York City was just enough. Bill and I were glad to find ourselves two hours later heading north on the New York State Thruway. We skipped the luncheon. Mordecai Potter was scheduled as keynoter—if he made it. I wonder what Mordecai Potter and José Moreno would say to each other. How about Bill Wittle and A. Sampson Wilson-Rallston? Imagine a school where José Moreno is principal, Potter and Wilson-Rallston are teachers, and all the toughest kids from Harlem are the students. How long would those guys survive as teachers? Maybe what we really need is a kind of a cultural revolution where all the professors of education, consultants, school superintendents, and education bureaucrats get farmed out to the public schools to harvest rice.

I shared this insight with Bill, who was driving. He felt the idea had possibilities, but added that in order to make it a truly valuable learning experience they should not be allowed to talk to each other about how to do their work. Make sure they're far enough apart and busy enough that they simply cannot talk with one another. Yeah, I said, and then pay 'em about half of what all the other peasants get. Yeah, said Bill, and make sure that whenever one of 'em comes up with an idea, he gets told it won't work. And make sure they all pick rice the same way, and give 'em more rows than they can possibly handle in a day. And then when they do a lousy job tell 'em it's their fault. And if they screw up, give 'em more rows.

And then tell 'em it's a noble profession.

5.

The Team Thing Debacle

We said it was the fault of the guidance director. The guidance director said it was the fault of the assistant principal for not adequately informing him. The assistant principal said it was the fault of the principal since she's supposed to be in charge. The principal said it was the fault of the new data systems director the district had hired to oversee things computer. The new data systems director said it was the fault of Computer Central, an outside contractor located in Oregon that prepares the master schedule each year. And Computer Central explained how they had a brand-new computer and they were just getting the bugs out. In other words, the trail of blame went this way: Jim, Bill, and Ellie blamed Al who blamed George who blamed Roberta who blamed Jane who blamed the people in Oregon who blamed the computer. Thus the trail of blame led, as it always does in the modern world, to increasingly distant persons and ultimately to technology. There were a few bugs to be gotten out.

There were, indeed.

After the principals' convention the previous May, the school year had wound to a close and summer vacation had come and gone with its usual speed. We'd returned to school the day after Labor Day excited and a little anxious about commencing our team-teaching project. But by the second week of September, our colleagues were in uproar over all the problems being caused by "the team thing." And hadn't they told us these problems would happen? They surely had. And wasn't it too late now to say we're sorry? It surely was. And weren't we really to blame for this mess because we'd started the ball rolling? That's right. We were.

What happened was we returned to school on the third day of September—two days before the kids—to take care of all those matters to which teachers must attend before kids return: set up bulletin boards, sharpen pencils, locate chalk and Scotch tape, run dittoes, attend meeting with department head, attend meeting with principal, attend meeting with union president, attend meeting with director of guidance, attend meeting with new districtwide health and safety coordinator, and attend meeting with superintendent. (I would really have liked to attend a meeting with the people in Oregon but that did not happen.)

Also included among these before-the-kids-return activities was the review of student lists, computer-produced sheets (from Oregon) with names of our new students printed alphabetically by section, five lists in all. Between meetings, I went to my mailbox to pick up my list. Ellie was doing the same, so we sat down together in the faculty lounge and compared lists. We looked first at our second- and third-period sections, classes that were supposed to have the same kids for our team project. My list began:

Alliger, Phillip
Andriano, Michael
Barone, Richard
Bauer, Melissa
DeMartino, Ralph

Ellie's list began:

Andriano, Michael
Caulfield, Marta
Coleman, Jerome
Conners, Raymond
DeMartino, Ralph

"Ellie," I said, "your list isn't the same as mine. You got the right one?"

"Third period," she said. "How 'bout you?"

"Second period." They were the right lists.

We compared the rest of our lists. Of twenty-three students in my class, Ellie had eighteen.

"Well, maybe they're in the other section," said Ellie, referring to the second of our paired groups. We looked. Of the eight students unmatched from the first group, three appeared in the second. We went to see Bill. We compared lists. More mismatches. Of our fifty-one students, there were thirteen who appeared in one of our classes (social studies, English, or home economics) but not the other two, and there were six students who appeared in two but not the third. We headed off to see Roberta.

Roberta was angry. She even said damn. Roberta rarely swears. She also said she'd straighten it out right away.

Two weeks later it was not straightened out. In fact, it was very unstraight, with baying hounds at every turn.

Bernice cornered me in the hallway one morning. "You know this team . . ."—she was searching for the right word—"this team . . . thing has really become quite a nuisance."

"What's the problem, Bernice?" I asked, feigning interest in hearing from the source what I already knew was going on.

"Well." Bernice wound up for her fast ball. "My second-period French 1 is severely underenrolled, to the point that it may be dropped. And I went to see Mr. Reynolds. Mr. Reynolds said that it was all due to this special project, this . . . this . . . (still couldn't find it) this team thing and how it just had a few minor glitches that had to be worked out. Glitches, my eye! This is all part of a larger scheme, don't you know, by administration to reduce personnel. You know that, don't you?"

Then there was the Admiral (Donald Rickover, social studies department chair). Don was usually amiable and not at all prone to the permanent state of flusterment characteristic of Bernice Fleischmann. But on the day in question, there was indeed considerable flusterment in his demeanor. I had been summoned to his office for a talk.

"I want you to look at something here, Jim." The Admiral pushed a paper in front of me as I sat down across from him at his desk, which was its usual jumble of scattered files, administrative memos, textbooks under review, and more. Somewhere way underneath it all was a blotter.

I looked at the paper. It showed departmental enrollments. He said, "I want you to look at the last three ninth-grade sections, there at the numbers. What do you see?" The numbers were big. All the manipulations required by the team thing had resulted in vastly larger sections for other teachers. Something we had promised would not happen. But I was not going to play along with the Admiral's socratic game.

"I know," I conceded. "It's an incredible mess, but Roberta is working on it and she says the guidance department is fully aware and is also working overtime to straighten it out."

Even as I spoke, the irony of my statement was playing itself out at the other end of the building. As Ellie later told me, she had gone to see Barry Pattison (guidance counselor) the same day about straightening out a couple of schedules for the team thing and had told Barry to be sure to not re-schedule any more students into the teamed classes without first checking with Roberta. "What teamed classes?" Barry had said. Hadn't he been told? Wasn't everybody aware? Apparently not.

What we have here is a failure to communicate.

But the worst of it was the effect all this was having on the kids. By the end of week two, at least a dozen students had

had their schedules changed twice, some even more than that. Because I now had a freshman homeroom, I could view first-hand the angst and general confusion all this was causing. On receiving her third new schedule in eight days, Gina Steffanelli declared, "I don't think my teachers like me in this school. They keep on trying to get rid of me." Richard Barone was less self-flagellating. "This school sucks. They can't even get the schedules right." Other similar comments were beginning to spring up here and there wherever freshmen gathered.

By the third week of school it was still not straightened out. It was time to put a stop to all the nonsense. Ellie, Bill, and I met. We decided that Al and Roberta and George and the new data systems director and Oregon had had long enough. It was time to ditch this thing. The three of us trudged down to Roberta's office and gave her the news that we were hereby quitting this project. Roberta was sympathetic and, especially after we told her what kids like Gina Steffanelli and Richard Barone were saying, agreed it was the right thing to do and she would inform the other administrators.

By the sound of O. J. Dave's memo, which arrived in Bill's, Ellie's, and my mailbox two days later, there must have been real fire and brimstone raining down at Central Admin. The memo directed us to appear at a meeting two days hence to "work out the means of continuing the Junior-Senior High School Team Pilot Project." Not only were we now being commanded to forward march, but we were also a Pilot Project. Apparently somebody at Central Admin had taken ownership of this baby and was in no mind to accept that the engine of this new, shiny, sexy sports car was seized up even as the car was rolling out of the showroom.

So we met. In O. J. Dave's large and (pressboard) paneled office. The whole crew: Assistant Principal George Handelman, Guidance Director Al Santorini, High School Principal Roberta Walters, Assistant Superintendent Dr. H. Frederick Latimer, Superintendent of Schools Dr. O. J. David McBrave, and the new Data Systems Director, Dr. J. Jane Lawson, plus Bill, Ellie, and me.

O. J. Dave began with some generally conciliatory remarks—he knew the three assembled teachers had taken some considerable heat from their colleagues for what was now being called the team thing debacle. He then commenced saying how really it was all his fault, and then Roberta, not wishing to be outdone, said it was her fault, and then it was Al's turn and Jane's and shortly everybody was taking responsibility for this unfortunate episode.

"But," said Dr. J. Jane Lawson, "we should not throw out the baby with the bath water." And with that, all eyes turned to us as if to say, we *are* moving ahead with this. All except Roberta, who among the administrators present was still close enough to daily school life and kids and teachers to know that ultimately we, as the persons who would have to carry this thing out in the classroom with our students, should be the ones to decide if and how this project would proceed. And at that moment, in a move of singular distinction, Roberta spoke. And she said that if we as the teachers felt that this all was not right, then we should make the decision to abort the project. For that, Roberta, the yet untenured principal, got the evil eye from more than one of her bosses, especially J. Jane, who was clearly the moving force behind this one.

Ultimately, we, the teachers, decided not to go ahead, which set most everybody on up the line to wringing their hands. But after all, they had to concede. We were in the driver's seat and they knew it.

There is an epilogue. Nearly a year after the team thing debacle debacled, a certain article in *Education World* magazine was brought to my attention. The article highlighted a trend in school districts toward the hiring of in-house specialists in data systems management. Among the school people interviewed was Dr. J. Jane Lawson, Data Systems Director in the Amesley Central School District in New York State where, according to the article, everything from cafeteria menus to the scheduling of interdisciplinary teaching teams was being electronically coded and beamed out to a mainframe computer in Oregon. Judging by the broad smile spread across J. Jane's face, this had been a predebacle interview.

The undoing of the team-teaching project at Amesley, though particular to Amesley High School, is typical of failed ventures in innovation in so many public school settings. The problem is that there are just too many opportunities for innovation to go wrong. If it's not the computer, it's the computer programmer, or somebody using either as a scapegoat. Or there are state regulations against it. Or the scheme gets fouled up in a turf squabble between departments. Or the teachers' contract won't allow it. Or the board of education gets a case of cold feet. The list goes on.

I was fed up with the system. It would never change. So I had a choice. Either become an education terrorist and sabotage the system or just do the best I could with things as they were. Being basically a family man, I chose the latter. For the next three months I didn't make no waves. No speeches, no committees, no memos, no revolutionary-type meetings. No team teaching, no letters to the editor, no heated exchanges with colleagues over coffee, no applying for grants, no conferences, no reading about Innovation in the Schools. And I stopped hanging around Bill, whose cynicism, ever since the team thing debacle, had become more than just a pragmatic style, a way of coping, a way of psychologically brokering high ideals (which Bill held) and less than ideal circumstances. It seemed to have infected his blood. He'd stopped caring about kids. The remarks he'd previously reserved for "the system" were increasingly directed toward his students. He was burning out. And he wouldn't listen to me or anyone else who was attempting with increasing directness to point this sad fact out to him. So I did what self-preservation dictated I should do. I stopped listening to Bill, I closed the door to my classroom, I ignored the bureaucratic monsters and demons that arrived in the form of memos and invitations to join committees, and I taught my kids.

*   *   *

"Jason, do *not* throw Abdula's purse out the window. In fact, Jason, close the window, give Abdula's purse back to Abdula, take your seat, and then see me after class."

Abdula was an Afghani refugee whose family had somehow made it to the United States via Pakistan. Life at Amesley High was different from the Moslem world and different again from a war zone—certain similarities notwithstanding—so Abdula was doing her best to adjust. She'd never had a male teacher and certainly never had male classmates. When she appeared at my door in mid-October in the company of Bob Reynolds, who attempted an introduction, it quickly became clear that her English was no better than my Farsi (her native language). Bob left and we were on our own.

Initially, the rest of the class was very offput by Abdula's veil—not a full veil, just a colorful handkerchief that went over the top of her head. Her face was in full view. After a while, though, some of the girls started to warm to her. The turning point came, I think, on the day of her first run-in with Jason, who tried to remove her veil just as class was starting. Abdula turned like a whip, slapped Jason full in the face and called him a "cocksucker motherfucker," which came out "coogsookah moothahfookah." In unison, the class went, "Whoa!" I moved Jason and spoke with both of them after class and later with Jason alone about how cultures are different, and respect, and how if he did it again I'd nail his head to the floor. The last part impressed him most. After that, Abdula began to get the attention of some of the girls in class and her English vocabulary expanded. Jason pretty much left her alone, which is why his purse snatching discouraged me. Two steps forward and one backward.

Altogether, period six was an interesting class. Twenty-six students in ninth-grade social studies. Besides Abdula, there was Paul. Paul was a very nice kid who happened to have cerebral palsy and was wheelchair-bound. His speech was barely discernible and his arms and legs so affected by the palsy that they were held to his side in braces that looked like oarlocks around his wrists and calves. He seemed still to have some control over his left wrist and used it to control a toggle switch that moved his wheelchair. By virtue of a very committed family (I'd met his parents before school started), a tape recorder that he used for class notes, and his own extraordinary persistence, he had a B+ average.

And there was Frederick, who'd joined us in October. I knew he'd been involved with the courts because periodically I had to fill out forms commenting on his behavior and progress in class. But it wasn't until November that Bob Reynolds, his counselor, mentioned, just by the way, that he'd been convicted of armed robbery and was on probation.

Oh.

And there were twenty-three other students, some of whom were no doubt also coming from extraordinary circumstances that I just happened to be unaware of and all of whom were distinct individuals whose individuality ideally should be appreciated and understood by me, their teacher, but unfortunately was not. Every now and then, I got glimmerings, but by and large they were just a mob—a nice mob, but a *mob* that arrived at my door every day at the same time and for whom I provided instruction, as per the system, of forty-five minutes. Sometimes I just wanted to scream, "These are kids, for godsake!" But railing against the system like that would be like yelling at my lawnmower for not starting—which I sometimes do—because the system is a system, not a person, and systems don't respond the way people do.

I thought about Bill Pierce's idea (Bill Pierce, who was finally getting crushed by the system) of reorganizing schools that had become the basis of our PAE report. And how we could be doing a lot more for kids without spending any more precious taxpayer dollars if we (people) just decided to take charge of the system for once.

Take Frederick. In addition to his regular classroom teachers, he met regularly with remedial teachers in writing and reading and math. Also, there were weekly meetings with his guidance counselor. Despite all this attention, there was no single adult at school who ever saw Frederick for more than forty-five minutes a day. There was a lot of busy activity by professionals who were there to address Frederick's skill deficiencies and emotional problems and academic needs and so on, and on the face of it, the system was laboring mightily to compensate all those disadvantages that collectively made Frederick what the system calls an at-risk kid. And, indeed, there was no lack of concern on the part of any of those professional educators, who in their forty-five minutes with Frederick (who was just one of many kids with whom each of those professional educators worked) labored minutely even as the system labored mightily to help Frederick. But somehow it was just a lot of busywork because nobody was really reaching Frederick either academically or personally, because reaching someone means getting to know someone and getting to know someone takes time, sustained periods of time, and flexibility and so on, and you know how to finish this paragraph.

It doesn't have to be this way.

Kids do mature. Maybe despite the system and our misguided efforts. By December, sixth period was showing they could write a decent essay and engage in a serious discussion without all talking at once. And Jason, despite his setback with the purse incident, was showing signs of tolerance. (He kicked Allen for making fun of Abdula's accent one day.) So I decided to try something different: my resolve to close the door and just do what was expected of me was weakening.

My mind kept going back to that UN conference I attended every year—the one that was entirely student run and kids learned so much and nobody talked about grades and how it happened outside of school time. And that made me think about how most good education occurs outside of school time. And then I thought about my ninth-graders, who were indeed maturing, and how they were languishing in all these classes that we throw at them. And so I thought, why not try to run a UN conference during school time for all those ninth-graders at Amesley. And then I thought, no. It would be chaos. Kids running through the halls, screaming and yelling, classes disrupted, food flying everywhere, fist fights, and all with those school administrators looking on in cool horror.

Despite this last insight, I wrote up a very official-looking proposal a full nine pages long and gave copies to Roberta, the Admiral, and Janet Degen, who had the other ninth-grade sections of GLOBSTU9R. Unfortunately, they all thought it looked like a pretty decent idea. Which meant of course that despite the aforementioned vision of flying food, etc., etc., we were now under the gun to actually go ahead with it.

It would be a two-week unit, we decided. During most of that two weeks, class time would be devoted to teaching kids about the UN, training them in debate procedure, and getting them started on research into UN-type issues that they would address. The project would culminate at the end of two weeks with a long conference. In the morning, kids would meet in committees of about twenty and then in the afternoon all resolutions that passed the committees would be brought to the general assembly, in which all 137 freshmen would participate, for further debate and a final vote. It could work, but orchestrating it would be a trick.

One potential obstacle would be locating six teachers who would agree to supervise the morning committee sessions. Even more daunting, we'd have to approach the entire faculty with the idea, since it meant disrupting all freshman classes for an entire day. This last item was accomplished with greater ease than I expected. The only disruption caused by our program would take place on that final day for the morning committee sessions and the afternoon general assembly. While it would be extraordinary to ask that all freshman classes be suspended on that day so that we could conduct our UN program, it would not be extraordinary to announce that all freshmen would be going on a field trip—only this field trip would take place on site. Thus, an "in-house" field trip. It served our needs and the rest of the school went for it.

Learning is hard to measure. The best kind of learning—the kind that stays with you the rest of your life—is maybe impossible to measure. This is a source of great frustration to small minds that are compelled to measure all and discard all they cannot measure. But for teachers, it is a fact of life. Actually, it *is* a fact of life. Teachers recognize it for what it is. How much learning from our UN project stuck? In my judgment, lots. First of all, kids were excited. The day I announced we were going to be doing something different in class during the coming two weeks, the kids' energy level rose noticeably. When I told them classes would be suspended on the last day, they got really excited. And not just because they were going to miss math and French and biology (and social studies), although that was part of it, but because canceling classes sent a message to the kids that whatever was in store must be good if those teachers were willing to mess up that all-holy schedule to make it happen.

Anyway, the UN project worked. Here's one memorable exchange from the terrorism committee, which I supervised. On a gamble, I'd elevated Jason (of period six purse-snatching fame) to chairperson.

Jason: Chair recognizes People's Republic of China.

Jill: (*speaking as PRC delegate*) I don't like the idea that we're being called terrorists here. I mean, if we vote for this resolution, it means we're saying we're terrorists.

Allen: (*from Nigeria, and sponsor of the resolution*) That's because you are.

Jason: Whoa, wait a minute. You're talking out of turn. I haven't recognized you yet.

Allen: (*continuing to interrupt; appealing to Jason*) But they *are!*

Jason: I'm warning you, Nigeria. Remember, I could . . . (*pause as Jason tries to recall procedural term*)

Mr. Nehring: (*in stage whisper*) You could revoke his speaking privileges.

Jason: That's right, I could revoke your speaking . . .

Mr. Nehring: Privileges.

Jason: Your speaking privilege.

Allen: (*appealing to Mr. Nehring*) He can't do that.

Mr. Nehring: (*nods head "yes" without speaking*)

Allen: Harumph.

Jason: Chair recognizes Mexico.

Allen: Hey, I had my hand up.

Jason: Yeah, and I don't feel like calling on you.

Allen: Harumph.

Altogether, the students proceeded much as their adult counterparts might. After it was all over, reports began to filter in from the ninth-grade homeroom teachers that all the kids had talked about for the last week was who was on what committee and what resolutions were going to be debated and who was to be the chairperson and so on. It was all a great lesson in shared power, persuasive communication, and restraint (a tough one for ninth-graders). It was great.

When I've seen special projects like this undertaken by schools, they are, more often than not, a great success. I've seen whole schools organize a day around a theme such as the Renaissance. The kids get charged up, parents get involved, teachers who haven't spoken in years find themselves working together. Everyone pulls together and the memory lingers sometimes for years. The fact that these things succeed as well as they do ought to stir us into asking, how come we don't do them more often? The answers are predictable enough. We have to cover the syllabus. It takes too much work. We'd lose control of the kids. One day is okay, but you can't do it all year. Thus we slouch back into our accustomed mode.

*   *   *

So why *did* the team thing debacle? Here's why.

I took some kids on a field trip to New York City a couple years ago. I'd been helping Bill Pierce with the literary arts magazine and we'd promised to take the editorial staff to the Metropolitan Museum of Art if we made our final dead-line, which we did despite Ralph Peters's hemming and haw-ing over the appearance of an exposed female breast on page two. We and the kids argued it was a literary arts magazine for goodness' sake and the Greeks made nude statues and famous museums had a lot more than just exposed breasts hanging on their walls and they were after all open to the general public including high school kids who could just for the price of admission see multiple naked bodies male and female in a variety of poses so what harm was there in one exposed female breast on page two of our award-winning literary arts magazine, Ralph? Ralph said it was suggestive. Bill argued it suggested nothing at all; it was there for all to see. This did not help to sway Ralph, ever concerned about the reaction that might be provoked from the "more conser-vative elements of the community" (one element of which was Ralph). So we finally worked a compromise. The naked breast could appear, but it had to be reduced to half size and buried farther back in the book on the supposition that all those conservative elements would not find it way back there since they generally did not carefully inspect the literary arts magazine, anyway. But this is not the point of my story. It's the trip to New York, which is a kind of an allegory for school reform.

Bill could not go, so we rented a ten-passenger van and I drove. The ten-passenger van turned out to be a fifteen-passenger van with big Mickey Mouse–type side view mirrors that made the van a total of about a lane and a half wide, and there were five rows of seats in all, which produced the effect, once I had hoisted myself into the driver's seat and looked rearward through the Mickey Mouse side mirrors, of a stretch Greyhound bus.

The museum was fine and we all had a good time. We counted thirty-five exposed female breasts in all from eighteen individual works of art. The missing breast lay presumably at the bottom of the Mediterranean Sea, where it had broken from the rest of the statue sometime before the Greek fisher-man found it in his net one day in 1968. We all posited that in fact the Greek fisherman had found the statue intact but decided that justice should dictate that he get to keep one breast for himself. The real drama of the day, however, occurred in two installments. The first was finding a parking space.

Circling two city blocks, I summarily determined that street parking was out. My driver's license test had not included parallel parking a Greyhound bus. So it would have to be a garage. Only problem was, every garage that we passed had a big sign out front that said "No Vans." Finally, about twenty blocks from the museum, our editor-in-chief, Eileen Schwarz, spotted a parking garage that as best as we could tell had no "No Vans" sign posted anywhere. This, my students assured me, meant that they would accept vans. (This is an excellent example of kid logic, which reasons that in the absence of clear admonition assume permission.) There being no real alternative, I ventured in. At first, everything seemed okay—plenty of clearance all the way around. But as we ventured downward, the passage started to narrow. First, the walls closed in about a foot on each side. Then a bunch of pipes appeared on the ceiling, hanging down about six inches. Our antenna scraped. Eileen hopped out, scrunched the antenna down below the roof line of the van. Then the walls came in another six inches on each side. I was crawling downward, thinking that there would be only one thing worse than getting stuck in this pit, and that would be having to back out. Then the right side mirror scraped. I hit the brake. Eileen hopped out again and scrunched the mirrors in as close as they would come to the sides of the van. The kids were loving it. This was real theater-in-the-round. And what a great story it would make: how Mr. Nehring totaled the van on our field trip to New York City. Having now compressed our van to its smallest compact size, we proceeded again forward. Then a knob protruding from one of those immovable overhead pipes made a sudden entrance in the form of a loud scraping noise like fingernails on a chalkboard. Everybody in the van went *eeeaaaugh* (a sound hard to render in written English). I hit the brakes and Eileen said, "Look" and pointed to the ceiling of the van over her head, which was now ever so slightly concave. Against the unanimous protests of my passengers I decided to accept the worst, and started to back out. This decision led to a repeat of both the aforementioned scraping knob sound and the crowd reaction sound. Eileen volunteered to get out and guide me backward from behind the van. (I hope she never told her parents about all this.) To everyone's disappointment (except mine) we made it back to the street. After another half hour we located a parking space in a vacant lot where the supposed manager reluctantly agreed to forgo the "No Vans" policy after we agreed to pay double to park on his already overpriced rubble pile.

The other part of the story has to do with going home. Having agreed on our final breast count, we piled in the van and began the sojourn home. Unfortunately, it was 5:00 P.M. on Friday. I do not generally know my way around Manhattan, but I understood from directions that Bill had hastily given me the day before that from where we presently were (as best I could ascertain) we would have to go east, then north on whatever avenue happened to go that way, and then make a right turn and get on FDR Drive going north. It sounded relatively simple, and indeed it was. Except that, as I said, it was 5:00 P.M. on Friday and it seemed that approximately one fourth of all the licensed vehicles in Manhattan were attempting to follow the same route as Bill had described to me. The remaining three fourths were also on the road, evenly distributed in their direction of travel among the other three points of the compass. Forty-five minutes later we found ourselves aimed north on First Avenue exactly one block and, as it turned out, one and a half hours shy of the entrance ramp to FDR Drive. We were in the extreme left lane and not moving. Of course there was no lack of advice from my editorial staff, who were all talking and gesturing that I should move right, pull ahead, back up, anything but stay where I was, which, based on my assessment of things, seemed to be the only rational course of action, seeing as I was surrounded by surly-looking drivers in other vehicles that were also not moving. So we sat. We watched the light at the end of the block turn from red to green to red to green and so on (one of the kids who was making note of this lost count after forty-something red lights). We also observed how whenever the light turned red, there remained in the intersection a virtual blockade, three lanes wide. And then everybody traveling east would attempt, despite this formidable obstruction, to proceed eastward and some amazingly would make it while others amidst much horn blowing and screeching brakes would get stuck halfway through when the light turned red for them and green for everybody going north. Then everybody going north would get angry and honk their horns until the light turned again. As I said this happened well more than forty-something times. We finally got home.

Over every school in North America there should be a big sign that says "No Vans." The absence of such signs does not imply, as we discovered by way of our team-teaching experiment, that vans are permitted. The other moral of the story is that if we have achieved nothing else in public education, we've managed to get all licensed vehicles on the road at once, all headed in different directions so that nobody gets anywhere, resulting in a vastly uncoordinated system of public education that is hopelessly gridlocked.

I was glad that Model United Nations had turned out a big success. Only three of our colleagues complained and many others actually said we should do more of this kind of thing. I wanted to say we tried to do more of this kind of thing when we set up the team-teaching project, except that the system gagged on it and threw us up ("No Vans"). Model United Nations worked only because it was so small. It was an aberration that the system could tolerate because it lasted only one day.

The system.

About this time I began to conclude—*really* conclude as the result of logical thought, not just whine as the result of downtroddenness—that the system was incapable of change, that it was like New York City at rush hour on Friday, that all opposing forces canceled each other out, that the system was at rest. Assuming that, I began asking myself, how should we then proceed? Should we (a) accept things as they are; (b) dismantle the system (Jerry Rubicon's vouchers); or (c) do something else?

In the midst of my ruminations, Lithuania declared independence. Having located Lithuania on the map, and having learned to distinguish it from Estonia and Latvia (Lithuania sounds like lithium, which is a metal, and metals are heavy, sinking to the bottom; therefore Lithuania is the southernmost of the three republics), I decided to have a current events discussion. Before class, I wrote on the board, "Lithuania Declares Independence." Then, under that, "So what?" Period one sauntered into the room. Period one usually sauntered. It wasn't just a sleepy shuffle, it being first period and my eleventh-graders being not quite awake yet. It was a definite saunter. There was defiance in it, as if to say, I got out of bed for this, it better be good. At the bell, I asked the class to respond to what was on the board. They agreed. I then pointed out that neither sentence was a kind with which one should agree, and rather that the second sentence in particular was intended to provoke a more complex response. Still, they agreed. So I said, "Well, there must be some significance to it. I mean, why do you think the editors down there at the *Union-Gazette* decided to put this story on the front page and to give it"—I went over to my desk drawer and pulled out a ruler—"a one-inch headline? I mean, it's not every day that you see a big banner headline like this."

"Maybe it was a slow news day," said Sarah from behind an elaborately colored tie-dyed T-shirt.

"Okay." It was clearly time to up the ante. "Everybody up out of your seat. School's canceled. Go stand against the wall."

"Huuh?" they intoned sleepily.

"You heard me. Let's go. Everybody go stand against that wall over there."

"You gonna shoot us?" asked Jeff.

Slowly, skeptically, they complied. As they did, they started to appear less like the living dead and more like sixteen-year-old kids. "Okay, Sarah and Jeff, you're captains.

You get to choose sides for a softball game. The winning team gets five hundred dollars."

"No shit?" said Aaron. Jeff elbowed him.

"This is dumb," said Sarah.

"Come on," I said. "Play along. What else are you gonna do?"

Sarah started. "Okay, Alex, you're on my team." Alex flexed his arm muscles Atlas style and walked over toward Sarah.

"I get Bill," said Jeff.

They continued picking sides. Meanwhile, I was trying to figure out where all this was going to lead. When they got to the twenty-third and final kid, Teige Simpson, who was small, wiry, and very bright, they started to argue, as teams usually do at this point, over who should be burdened with this obvious liability. Jeff got him. Having been the smallest kid in the sixth grade myself, and having experienced exactly what Teige was now feeling, I empathized greatly. At that moment, I got an idea for what to do next.

"Okay, teams, go to opposite sides of the room and take a seat. Sarah and everybody over here. Jeff, your team over here." The teams went and sat at desks on opposite sides.

"All right, we're gonna change the rules. Instead of playing softball, it's gonna be a chess tournament, and instead of five hundred dollars, it's gonna be a million."

"Wait a minute. You can't do that." Jeff protested. "You're changing the rules in the middle of the game."

"And furthermore," I continued, "Teige, I want you to pick three people from your team, anyone you want, and you guys can be your own team and compete for the million dollars yourselves."

Teige's face brightened considerably. In no time, he raided Jeff's softball team of its best chess talent.

"Whoa, wait a minute, this sucks," Jeff protested.

"What's the matter, Jeff?" I said. "You upset that Teige bolted and took some of your best talent?"

"No, wait a minute. You just don't do that."

"Lithuania did," I said.

"That's different," said Sarah.

"What's the difference?" I asked. No response, so I continued. "Lithuania decided they wanted to bolt from the Soviet Union. You guys thought it was no big deal. Now we play a stupid game, and you guys are about to strangle me because I break up your team."

"Yeah, but you changed the rules halfway through," said Alex of the large biceps.

"Well," I said, "for the Soviet Union, the game used to be called the Cold War, but that's been changed in the last few years. Now it's called economic competitiveness and keeping up with the Japanese. Gorbachev himself has changed the rules. It's called perestroika."

So our little current events discussion was off and running. We all learned where Lithuania is on the map—I told them about Lithuania and lithium, which they said was dumb—and learned about the history of the Baltic republics, including the Treaty of Brest-Litovsk and Joseph Stalin and all the rest. By the time we were done, it seemed most people were rooting for little Lithuania, except for Jeff, who felt strongly that the Soviet Union had a right to roll the tanks into Vilnius and quell the rebellion.

All of this served to crystalize my thinking about school reform. If Lithuania could do it, why not us? In the absence of something extreme like a voucher system, there was no way all of public education would change, but no way were we going to accept things as they were. So why not cut loose and do our own thing? The mother country could go along its merry way, but we would attempt to change our little corner of the world. The risk, of course, was that it might turn out like Prague Spring, but for the moment, a new spirit of independence was born.

Go, Lithuania!

6.

Bring on the Revolution

So I decided to pull together some of our ideas from the PAE committee report and write an article for the editorial section of the Sunday paper suggesting an experimental school program. Maybe if I threw the idea out to the community at large it would gather momentum. The article began this way:

> Here's an idea for a reformed high school. Take eight educators of varied expertise. Give them a budget, a secretary, adequate classroom space, and a list (no longer than a page) of broadly defined areas of knowledge that their students should possess in order to receive a diploma. Assign them one hundred students for four years. Then turn 'em loose.

The rest of the article basically talked about what a great idea it was and how it was realistic and doable despite the fact that it violated probably a score of state education regulations.

They ran it on Sunday, April 1.

Within a week I'd received over one hundred letters of support. The phone rang constantly. Eventually Laurie and I stopped answering it and we racked up a record thirty-five messages on our answering machine. The state commissioner of education arrived at school later in the week to congratulate me personally and offered me assistance in any way he could. The Ford Foundation sent a letter offering $50,000 seed money and asked if it would be enough. The board of education voted unanimously to donate the central administration building as space for the new school and O. J. Dave agreed to move Central Admin's operations to a tent out back.

Then I woke up. Actually, the response *was* fairly encouraging. The absence of letter bombs was a good sign. So was the fact that no official action was taken by either the board of education or the state education department to keep me from practicing my chosen profession. One student said he saw my name in the paper. When I asked what he thought, he said he hadn't known my first name was James. Also, I observed no visible change in the way most of my colleagues treated me (none of the post-team-thing-debacle-type dirty looks or heated exchanges). Tuesday at lunch I made a series of increasingly blunt allusions to the article without any sign of recognition so finally I just came right out and asked if anyone had seen my piece in the paper.

Bob Reynolds said, "Your what?"

Andy Murdoch said, "You pissed on the paper?"

"I think he means he needs a piece of paper," offered Janet Degen.

There was, after all, some small show of support. I received a phone call from Jason's mother, Jason the former purse snatcher and veil puller who, ever since the UN program, had turned over a new leaf. She called to say she wanted to talk about . . . about just school. She was having a hard time with this conversation. She said she'd never called a teacher like this (she had called me at home), but that she just felt that schools ought to be different somehow. Between her halting manner and her confession that school ought to be different "somehow," she won my complete trust and confidence. I told her that I, too, lacked certainty about just how schools ought to be different, but shared her conviction that they weren't right as they were. That seemed to put her at ease. We talked a long time—well, an hour anyway—about school and kids, and how teachers could teach better and how parents could be better parents.

Mrs. Westerfield gave me an insight that really stuck. She said that a parent sends a child to school uncomfortable with the knowledge that school will not provide the same attention and support that the child receives at home. (This is a well-founded feeling.) As the child moves inevitably upward through the grades, the amount of individual attention he or she receives decreases. By the time the child reaches high school, the gulf has widened almost immeasurably. At home a child is one of maybe two or three other children under the care of one or two adults. At school, the child competes with a hundred-plus individuals for the attention of any one of their teachers. This is why parents regularly beat up on teachers for not understanding and not paying enough attention to their kids (they don't) and why teachers beat up on parents for asking the schools to do too much. Both sides are coming from different realities.

We were becoming fast friends. She said she knew people around town who felt the same way and who would be very interested in seeing some kind of experimental program set up, and not just for troubled kids or gifted kids but for anybody who just wanted a different kind of school experience. Then she asked where to next. I told her I wasn't sure but that if she really felt strongly, she ought to talk to a board member or two and see how they felt. I told her I'd let her know if anything developed at my end.

About this time Grace Haber, English teacher, started having discussions with her sophomores about school reform as part of a unit on Elizabethan literature (English teachers do amazing things). They asked me to join them as guest since I'm always talking about school reform. Grace had been reading Paulo Freire and had taken to heart his view that education begins with an awakening of consciousness about one's position in the socioeconomic order of things. Her school-reform discussions were intended to get kids to think deeply and critically about school, the place where they spend so much of their time.

I arrived just as class was beginning, Grace motioned for me to take any of the several seats still vacant in the circle of desks where all sat, including Grace. Grace made some opening remarks to the effect that today Donna, Hal, and Peggy would present their paper on school reform and then Mr. Nehring and everyone else would critique it. Donna and Hal eyed each other warily. Peggy began, "Our report is called 'Death by Boredom.' Nothing personal, Mr. Nehring." I had been Peggy's teacher the previous year.

"No need to apologize. Go right ahead," I said.

"This title means that we think the number-one problem with school is boredom. And it's not just that we're spoiled like we want our oyster on a silver platter—that's what teachers always think when we say we're bored—it's just the way school is, it's boring. So today, in our report, we're going to talk about why it's boring. And Hal is going to talk first about too many facts." Peggy looked at Hal.

"Well, as an example about too many facts and all," Hal began, "in social studies right now we're doing all the kings and queens of Europe and we're supposed to memorize like Henry the Seventh and Louis the Ninth and Otto the Twenty-second and all this stuff and like we all know we're going to forget it all after the unit test, so why are we bothering to learn it? I mean, what does it have to do with our lives? Is it gonna help us get a job? So, anyway, there are too many facts. That's just one example." Hal looked at Peggy.

Peggy the organizer said, "Thank you, Hal. Now Donna will talk about how we don't have enough freedom."

Donna spoke. "Well, we did a survey and we found that a lot of people have jobs. We asked thirty students at Amesley and seventeen had after-school or weekend jobs. Now, like I have a job. I work at the Acme Drugstore on Hudson Avenue. When I'm there they have me handling lots of money and working with customers, and Thursday nights I'm supposed to close the store down and make the night deposit at the bank. And so I'm in charge and the McGruders who run Acme trust me to do all that.

"Okay," Donna continued, sweeping a long blond wisp off her face and behind an ear. "So I come into school after working an evening at the store where I have all this responsibility and I walk into Mrs. Fleischmann's class and I like have to ask to go to the bathroom. And I can't leave my seat without asking permission. And I get detention if I chew gum. So anyway, I mean, the point is in the real world they treat me like an adult, but at school they still treat us like we're in second grade. It's no wonder that we don't wanna come here." Donna looked at Peggy. "I guess that's it."

Finally, it was Peggy's turn to speak. "I'm going to talk about two things. First is how learning is a guessing game. It's like we never know what we're going to be tested on. There's all this reading, all these notes and handouts and stuff and the teacher says there's going to be a unit test at the end of the week and you feel like saying, 'So what's it on?' In fact I said that in Mr. Grossi's class and he like gave this jerky smile and said, 'Everything.' It seems to me that if there's something you want us to know, you ought to just tell us what it is and then spend the week explaining it and then test us on it. I mean I don't see what's so wrong about that."

Peggy looked down at her note cards and thought for a minute. Then she looked up. "And there's another thing. School is boring, which goes back to our first point. It's not that we're spoiled rich kids, which is what Mr. Grossi says, it's that what we do in school is basically just boring. I mean you know we sit in a chair for almost an hour, listening to some guy go on about stuff and we take notes and then we go to another class and we hear some other guy go on about stuff and we take more notes, and it's just all day long. I mean come on. Wouldn't you be bored? So, anyway, that's why students look so tired all the time. It's not 'cause they're worn out, it's 'cause they're worn down. They're bored."

Hal, Peggy, and Donna then gave their solution, which

boils down to letting kids come and go as they please, giving them complete choice over their course selections, and replacing the student desks with overstuffed chairs and couches. I was impressed with their analysis of the problems, but their solution was rather less penetrating. It really did not provide an alternative, it simply eliminated the necessity of appearing dutiful to the present system.

One voice has been noticeably absent from the chorus of school-reform literature: students. We hear from scholars and policy makers, task forces and think tanks, sometimes even teachers. But what about kids? What do kids think about school and all those school-reform ideas? It seems they're rarely asked. Well, I've asked, and what I hear is the same broad variety of opinion that I hear from adults. Opinions range from the system is fine, it serves us well (this opinion usually from kids who are doing well in school) to the system is terrible, blow it up (predictably from kids who are generally not doing well). Though kids' attitudes toward school tend to align with their degree of success, there are also a significant number of successful students who think schools ought to be otherwise.

What do we make of this? What I make of it is that if we were to use our students' opinions as the sole guide for school reform, we would *not* close down every school tomorrow, but neither would we persist with the same monolithic system of education that presently characterizes our schools. We would try to create some diversity to serve the diverse backgrounds and needs of kids. The basic disjuncture of American public education is that schools are all the same but kids differ. My session with Grace Haber's English class confirmed my growing conviction that whatever school reform ideas we embrace, the bottom line must be the establishment of greater diversity to serve the diverse needs of kids. I repeat: kids differ, but under the present system schools are essentially the same.

The student reports emboldened me to think seriously about the experimental-school idea. Not only was there a group of interested teachers, but at least some kids shared our discontent with the status quo, and they could be powerful allies. It was time to start thinking about strategy.

I found myself talking to Bill Pierce first. I had been quietly trying to persuade myself that Bill was no longer the man to start a revolution, but he was still my friend and the person at work whom I naturally turned to when I had something on my mind. Since an experimental school was on my mind, that is what I brought to Bill.

"Work through the union," said Bill with a big sigh of finality. He took off his reading glasses, rubbed his eyes, and leaned back in his swivel chair. He'd been reading essays in his classroom. The kids had left a half hour before and it was raining. You could hear the rain hitting the pebbly surface of the flat tar roof over our heads. It made quite a racket.

Bill gazed out the window a moment, then spoke, still looking out the window. "You know, every time we try to do something in schools it doesn't work. I don't mean just you and me. I mean anywhere. And the problem is there's no agreement on how decisions are to be made. And the problem is also that the most stable group in school, teachers, have so little official say over what goes on. So, if you're really serious about trying something new"—Bill paused and shifted his gaze from the window to me—"*again,* then before you come up with any plan, any program, lay out a decision-making process that involves the voice of the teachers. I don't just mean teacher input on some damn committee. I mean bottom-line decision-making power so that if the teachers think it stinks, they can say it stinks and put a stop to it."

"You mean a vote," I said.

"Right, a vote. If the board of education really wants an intelligent verdict on a new program before putting it in place, then they should let their teachers, whom they hired, render their collective, expert judgment upon it. A vote."

"But I thought Jerry said—"

"Rubicon is wrong on this one," Bill interrupted. "The problem is that for all the great plans for school reform, nobody has figured out yet how you get them up and running. Democracy is good enough for government, so why isn't it good enough for professional decisions in our school?" Bill leaned toward me and pointed his finger. "You get O. J.

Dave to agree *in writing* that no program will go ahead until the faculty approves it with a majority vote, and you'll be on the right track. That vote'll put pressure on people in all the right places. It'll keep 'em honest and it'll keep 'em involved."

"He'd never go for it," I said.

"He wants to see success. If you can convince him this is the only way success is gonna happen, he'll go for it. And build your support through the union first. If teachers smell administration initiative on this you'll be finished before you start. The union is the only place teachers have some real power, so that's where you begin."

I faced a dilemma. Whom do I go to first, the administrators or the teachers? With the team-teaching project, we'd gone first to the administrators. That touched off protest among the teachers. If we went this time to the teachers first, how would the administrators respond?

*   *   *

Meanwhile, elections for student senate were being held. Which proved to be instructive for my own little endeavor. Campaigning was more vigorous than I'd seen in years, which I think had something to do with the slate of candidates for president. On the extreme right was Walter Del Florio, who carried a briefcase and greased his close-cropped hair so it always looked slicked back. Two years before, when I'd had him as a freshman in English, Walter had made clear his views on education. The class had been preparing a debate on the First Amendment and student rights. The last two days they had been vigorously arguing, one side of the room against the other. I'll admit it was a little out of hand, but arguments were being made and heard and countered, and in their own freshman sort of way, the class was making nice progress. Then all of a sudden, just as his side of the room was responding to Amy Merriweather's impassioned plea from the other side of the room for complete First Amendment protection for students, Walter stood up. I had noticed that he had been stewing all period. He hadn't said a word and I could tell the disorderliness of the debate was getting under his skin. So, all of a sudden he stood up, banged his fist to the desktop, and cried out with oratorical flourish, "Stop it! Stop it, I say! Stop this madness! Do you hear?" Apparently nobody did, except me, because Walter's side of the room kept on jeering Amy's speech. Walter stood granite-like for a moment. The jeering went on. Walter sat down, expressionless. At the end of the year Walter told me I was the worst teacher he'd ever had. To which I replied that it takes all kinds, meaning both teacher and students, though I'm not sure he got my full meaning. Next year, Walter took to carrying a briefcase and word was he regularly submitted names of bathroom smokers to the main office. Walter's campaign slogan was "Order for Amesley" and I privately wondered if Bernice Fleischmann was making secret contributions to Walter's campaign.

Next were two middle-of-the-road candidates, Alex Murray and Beverly Stillman. Alex was swim team captain and had been a student senator since his freshman year. He had a reputation among teachers as a nice polite kid who did his work and had mostly good grades. His campaign was well organized and enjoyed strong support. He was a professional politician. Beverly was currently secretary of student senate and was working to get out the female vote. Her campaign stressed that not since 1973 had there been a female president of student senate. Her campaign slogan was "We shall be heard," the terminal *d* of "heard" was altered to look like the female symbol. Beverly, too, had all the trappings of a mainstream politician: good grades, neat dress, reputation as a nice kid, and a résumé of student government involvement stretching back to the seventh grade.

Then there was Peter. Peter Baxter. Peter was very bright, got high grades without putting in a great amount of effort, and had no experience in student government whatsoever. He was articulate and irreverent. He read a great deal on his own and ran what he called a noncampaign for "The Do-Nothing Candidate." His posters showed a huge likeness of himself neatly dressed and smiling (Peter generally let his shirttails hang out and wore cut-off jeans). Large block letters across the bottom of the poster declared, "The Do-Nothing Candidate."

Peter's campaign was flawless. He handed out buttons in homeroom, wore a tie and jacket to school every day of the week before the election, and took to making vacuous political remarks like "We must restore pride in the community spirit" and "The time has come for action to speak louder than words" and "United we will overcome all obstacles."

Several days before the election, it was discovered that Peter had secretly been trying to organize a student union, an organization completely unaffiliated with the school, made up entirely of students and dedicated to representing student interests. Its separateness from school oversight would give it credibility and Peter's vision of it as a kind of labor union that would negotiate with school authorities suggested it could be a truly powerful organization.

This, of course, made the school authorities mighty nervous. Except for Roberta Walters. Privately, she told me she admired Peter, but O. J. Dave had given her the word from the board that this was unacceptable. So Roberta called Peter into her office and tried to persuade him to stop. This did not work. Partly because Roberta did not try very hard since she so admired the kid and partly because their little chat was just a good indication to Peter that he was hitting some pressure points, exactly what he'd hoped to achieve.

Finally, the day of campaign speeches arrived. Everybody piled down to the auditorium to hear all the candidates make their best pitch. Even Dr. McBrave was there. All would vote the next day in homeroom. Speeches were predictable. Walter Del Florio promised order in the hallways and clean bathrooms amidst much catcalling. Alex and Beverly recited their résumés and promised to not make promises they could not keep. Then came Peter, "The Do-Nothing Candidate." Peter did not give a speech, he gave a performance, a skit. The cast included a board member, the superintendent, the principal, and a certain fictional student who wanted to start a student union. The crowd cheered wildly as Peter finished. I glanced at O. J. Dave. He sat stone-still, calculating.

Just then, loud popping sounds rang from the front of the auditorium. There was commotion in the front row. The popping continued. Between the still-lingering cheers for Peter's speech and the fact that students were now getting out of their seats and beginning to leave the auditorium, it was hard to discern what exactly was going on. I pushed my way down the center aisle toward the front, against traffic. The popping continued but had slowed down some. Halfway to the stage, I stood on tiptoes and saw what it was. A pack of firecrackers had apparently been exploding and dancing wildly across the floor in front of the stage. When I got to the front, there were other teachers already there checking if everybody was okay. Everybody was. The students seemed amused. We were not.

To make a long story short, it was discovered that Peter's campaign manager had thrown the firecrackers in symbolic protest of school-sanctioned student government. Peter denied vehemently that he had anything to do with it. (I believed him. I think he had more sense than that.) His campaign manager was suspended from school, and Peter's name was stricken from the ballot. Jerry Rubicon was then called in to a meeting with McBrave, at which time he was told never again to counsel students in illegal activity and a letter of reprimand was placed in his personnel file. The district had picked the wrong scapegoat for this one. Jerry was furious. It seems Peter had come to Jerry with the idea of a student union some weeks before and Jerry had told him that an independent student organization would truly be a powerful body but that he could not advise them if they were really going to do it independently of the school. That was it. Jerry made the letter of reprimand publicly known to the faculty, grieved it, and ultimately won.

Peter Baxter got 18 percent of the vote on write-in.

Prague Spring.

Bearing all this in mind, I determined I should proceed cautiously with the experimental-school proposal. I informed the union leaders that I wanted to make a presentation at the next high school union meeting two weeks hence. They said fine, at which point I began the first of what was to become about ten different drafts of my speech. If we were really going to start a new school, I had to anticipate every possible obstacle, of which there would be many. The more I wrote, the more obstacles I thought of. My immediate goal was to persuade the teachers that this was a sound idea, which it was. There would be two main selling points. First, the proposal laid out a democratic decision-making process: no plan would be implemented until it received a majority vote of approval from the faculty. Second, it placed innovation at arm's length. In an experimental school, innovation could become at the same time more radical *and* less threatening. Since the experimental school would be more or less cut loose from the conventional high school, its altered programs would not have the same kind of disastrous ripple effect that the team thing had had. At the same time, those of us who were to be involved could really make significant departures from conventional school practice without fear of unsettling other programs. But others would be free to copy our successes, and all would learn from our failures.

Philosophy was easy. It's the politics that are daunting. So I gave a speech around the middle of April to twenty-one assembled union members (not bad, actually; union meetings usually drew four or five), having distributed a flyer describing the proposal to everyone's mailbox a week earlier. All this was to be followed up with a survey of faculty interest. The survey was conducted and, as it turned out, a majority of the faculty said they either favored the proposal or were neutral. Revolutions have succeeded with less. I was elated.

*   *   *

"O. J. Dave is really pissed," said Roberta, leading me into her office. She swung around behind her desk and gestured for me to sit.

"Uh-oh," is all I said, and sat. Roberta's remark was alarming for at least two reasons. First, it's generally not a good idea to get the superintendent of schools upset at you, especially when you're trying to persuade him of the rightness of your cause. Second, and even more unsettling, was Roberta's unusual abruptness. Roberta never said "O. J. Dave" and she never said "pissed." Actually, Roberta seemed to be getting more abrupt in general these days, and I was starting to wonder if something was up.

"Your little survey really floored him," Roberta continued. I'd written a letter requesting a meeting with the administrative team. "He seems to think you really went around him and said how it was conniving and unprofessional."

"Dr. McBrave said I was conniving?"

"And he also said the union has no business taking part in curricular issues. It exists strictly to negotiate wages and working conditions."

My mouth opened ever so slightly, anticipating that there should be something I would say at about this point. Roberta paused, also expecting some sort of statement from me. But nothing came out. So Roberta spoke.

"Well, I guess I stuck my neck out for you," she said.

"What did you do?"

"I convinced Dr. McBrave to at least hear you out."

"So there's gonna be a meeting?"

"Sort of." Roberta said and leaned forward in her chair, fiddling with a paper clip on her blotter. "*We're* having a meeting, but he won't be there. He'll be sending Fred to take part on his behalf; he said he's got other commitments. You're supposed to bring anyone who's interested and the meeting's supposed to be at four-thirty."

So O. J. Dave was pissed. Just like he was probably when Peter Baxter tried to organize a student union. I suppose I should've taken it as a good sign. If McBrave was upset, it was only because the security of his own authority was being challenged. I had to convince him that he was facing a movement and that it was therefore in his own best interest not to fight it but to embrace it enthusiastically.

Yeah, right.

More than half the battle of school reform is the internecine struggles of supposed allies within education: teachers, administrators, school boards, parents. Perhaps because public schools must be all things to all people, we fight so among ourselves. Anyway, I like to think it is more than just pride and fear, more than just résumé building and job security. Either way, though, the conflict is unavoidable. With the team-teaching project I'd gone first to the administrators, and teachers were upset. With the experimental school idea, I was going first to the teachers and now the administrators were upset.

I therefore had to make sure that a maximum number of people showed up for the meeting. I began a serious program of persuasion, importuning likely and sometimes not so likely individuals to please attend this meeting and to sign up on the roster I'd posted in the faculty room. The *roster?* Yes. I needed people who'd be willing to make a statement, and signing a roster would be a good first step.

"Lane, any chance you could come to the experimental-school meeting?" Lane Swanson, a career math teacher known to his colleagues as Memory Lane because he was always telling tales from the Old Days of Amesley, was an amazingly placid individual whose exterior masked a deeply thoughtful personality. We were waiting in line for the copy machine, which was jammed. Joe Grossi was kneeling before it in his accustomed cursing mode, flipping levers back and forth and extracting chewed-up, ink-stained pieces of paper.

"When is it?" Lane asked.

"Next Monday."

"Now what is this proposal all about again?" Lane asked tentatively.

"Well," I began, "it's a proposal that the teachers union and the district work together to create a kind of laboratory high school where innovative ideas can be tried out without boluxing up the whole system."

"Oh yes," said Lane. "I support that. Kind of like the old lab schools that used to be connected with colleges where you'd have ongoing research."

"Pretty much," I said, thinking to myself that wasn't *exactly* it because I knew that clicking through Lane's very scientific brain right now were concepts like control group and standard deviation and experimental design and hypothesis and the rest and that wasn't quite what I envisioned but it was close.

"If you can come," I continued, "I've got a roster over there." I pointed to the wall with the sign-up sheet.

"Yeah, I can come," said Lane.

Same day, I was walking down the hall to the main office and ran into Mary Price, guidance counselor, who was on hall duty.

"Jim," she called as I approached, "what's this meeting?"

I stopped and began to explain. "Well, it's kind of a place where we can try some really serious innovation without having to revamp the whole high school all at once." And so on.

"Oh," Mary said. "So it could be a kind of a place where kids who don't quite fit into the system could go and succeed instead of just dropping out?"

"That's one possibility," I said. Again it wasn't quite the way I conceived it, but still it was close.

"I'll be there," said Mary.

And thus I roamed the highways and byways of our fair school calling individuals unto the meeting. And lo, by Friday there were seventeen names on the roster. Number seventeen was Joe Grossi.

The experimental school had a different sort of appeal for Joe, as I found when I asked him about it.

"You know, Joe," I said as we walked down the sophomore hall. Our paths had met accidentally. "I remember how upset you and others were when the team thing was announced."

"Uh-huh," Joe said a little warily.

"I want you to know that the experimental-school proposal *requires*—bottom line—that the teachers vote to approve it before anything gets implemented."

"Oh yeah?" Joe's interest was piqued.

"That's the whole idea. We get a written agreement with the district in advance guaranteeing that kind of a decision-making process."

"Hmm," Joe intoned in a staccato way that means "not bad."

I decided to hit him between the eyes. "Can you come to the meeting?"

"What meeting?" The wariness returned.

"It's a meeting where we will formally present our proposal to the administrative team. It's at four-thirty on Monday."

"Christ almighty, four-thirty?!" Joe looked at me, then turned away. "I'll think about it."

Monday poured rain all day. There was a thunderstorm watch in effect for the evening and most after-school sports events had been canceled. Roberta stopped by my room after last period and said Fred had called to ask if the meeting had maybe been canceled. I told Roberta to tell Fred *we'd* be there. Roberta detected the annoyance in my voice and gave me a thumbs-up from the doorway before she turned to leave. Could this thing ever really succeed if we didn't have administrative support? The administrators have so much power. They not only control the budget, they know what the budget is—information generally not fully known to staff—and that knowledge alone gives them power. They can manipulate the budget to their own ends. They also have a direct line to the board of education—again, something we do not have. We are always told that our concerns are fairly represented in executive sessions but who knows how events are characterized and what kind of a spin is put on issues. Jerry Rubicon told me once that unless you have strong administrative support for an idea, you're dead in the water.

On the other hand, administrators really have very little power. The central-office administrators work at the pleasure of the board. If they disagree too much, they're history. Which means that a superintendent is in one sense a high-paid gofor, a yes-man. At the same time, administrators are constrained by their teachers, who though lacking official veto power have numerous unofficial ways of making their displeasure known, not the least of which is letting it out to the community. O. J. Dave once confided to me that unless you have faculty support, you're dead in the water.

Finally, it was nearly 4:30 on Monday. The seventeen names from the roster all materialized around the big table in Conference Room A—good people, all good for their word. Roberta was there, too. She was making some jovial small talk with Joe Grossi (Joe Grossi, of all people!) about cholesterol and how food with cholesterol really was not the problem, it was saturated fat. A definite change had come over Roberta in recent weeks. She was much more serene, almost to the point of devil-may-care. Bill Pierce was there, too. And Jerry Rubicon; it was reassuring to have the union big gun in the room. Janet Degen was there and Ellie Grosshartig. Not present was Bernice. Thank goodness.

At precisely 4:30, Assistant Superintendent H. Frederick Latimer, wise and skeptical Fred, walked into the room. He looked around and tried not to appear shocked by the number of people present, but his shock was nonetheless apparent. Then I noticed: there were no seats left. By coincidence we had the exact number of people to use up all the chairs. It was already clear that Fred didn't especially want to be here; there was no need for him to feel unwelcome, too. I offered him my chair and left the room to get another next door.

I returned, settled myself, and there was a little bit of an awkward silence. I then realized they were waiting for me. It hadn't occurred to me until that exact moment that, having called this meeting, it was up to me to get it underway. So I launched in. I had a little ten-minute speech, and that was as far as I had thought in terms of agenda. So I spoke, and it seemed like people were listening. And then there was Fred, who I know was listening because he was writing down every word. At one point I experienced a mental leap in which I was at a dismissal hearing (mine) and Fred was saying, "Did you not on April the seventeenth, state at a district meeting that . . ."

So anyway, I finished and then said something like, "Well, that's the proposal. We hope the administrative team will consider it and let us know your decision. Fred, are there any questions I can answer for you?"

"Lots," Fred said.

So we talked. And talked some more. Finally, Fred said we'd be hearing from them.

Three weeks later I hadn't heard anything. There having been two board meetings during that time. I began to feel our project was being neglected. My several phone calls to O. J. Dave's office were greeted with his secretary's cheery reply that Dr. McBrave was at work on it and would report as soon as they made a decision.

Other, more pressing matters, no doubt.

Every spring, usually a Saturday in May, the people on the street where I live have a block party. It's a wonderful old-timey gathering of neighbors who, having been isolated by snow and cold weather all winter, are eager to share news and renew acquaintances. The road gets blocked off to traffic and we set up picnic tables in the street for the food contributed potluck-style by all families attending. There's usually a lively game of kickball as well as horseshoes, which regularly draws its circle of aficionados, and just plain lawn chair sitting and talking in clusters of foldable chairs that sprout like huge springtime blossoms on front lawns. Being May, there's often still a chill in the air, which means that most of the adults wear sweaters, while most of the kids, eager to push the season, are stripped down to T-shirts and shorts. It's a wonderful piece of small-town Americana, and Allen Jaworski, who lives at the other end of the street and serves on the local school board, usually attends.

I knew Allen to say hi to and we'd had just a handful of conversations over the years, some of which were about school, but those tended to be very surface discussions as we were both fearful that we might convey some information that we would later find out we were not supposed to have conveyed and then get verbally abused by our peers for having conveyed it. This fear was, no doubt, greater than circumstances warranted.

Bearing all this in mind, I maneuvered my way over to the horseshoe area (Paul and Betty Jessup's back yard) where Allen was standing, beer in hand, next to Betty Jessup. They were talking casually and watching the horseshoe match in progress. I ambled up and offered in the most neighborly small talk sort of way I knew, "So, are you two the retired horseshoe champions?"

At which Betty shrieked, "Oh my god, the ice cream!" and hastily headed off toward her back door. Allen and I looked at each other a little confused.

"I have that effect on women," I said.

Allen chuckled. Then, looking off toward the sound of a horseshoe that had just clinked against the stake not far from where we were standing, he said, "So, Jim Nehring, how are things at Amesley High these days?"

Thankful that he had just spared me from further strategizing and just barely suppressing a smile that would reveal my glee, I answered, "Really well, actually. I'm very excited about the experimental-school idea."

"Ringer!" cried Allen and applauded. His wife, Helen, had just thrown up her arms exultantly over her good toss.

"That's good, Jim," said Allen vaguely. "I'm sorry, what did you say?"

"I say I'm excited about the experimental-school proposal."

"The what?"

"The . . . experimental . . . school . . . proposal."

"Oh now, what's that?"

"I thought Dr. McBrave had discussed it with you," I said.

"Not that I remember," said Allen. "Go ahead. Tell me about it."

So I told him the whole thing. I gave him the history of the PAE committee and the team thing debacle. I told him about how there was support in the union and how union-district collaboration could work to everyone's favor and how we needed to create opportunities for entrepreneurship and new ideas in education, and how we would seek outside funding and how it would possibly not cost the district very much. He seemed to like the last point especially well and said if O. J. Dave did not bring it up at the next meeting, he would.

A week and a half later, I got a call from O. J. Dave's secretary with a message from Dr. McBrave: if the union wanted to, the district would be willing to put together an agreement to start work on a cooperative venture for an experimental high school, and I should set up a meeting.

That day, also, Roberta told me confidentially that she'd submitted her resignation. She said she was "tired of the bullshit" and had taken a management position with a company in the area. She'd be making a lot more money, she said.

7.

Signing Out

And, lo, it came to pass that an agreement was reached in June by the union president and the superintendent of schools laying out a process to investigate the creation of an experimental high school. And unto this agreement were added numerous clauses stating in all manner of ways that teachers would vote on the plan before it became fixed upon the face of the district. And the teachers did consent to the agreement, and so did the board of education. And thus it was signed.

I like June. It is a time when the burden for learning shifts from teacher to student—where it rightly belongs all the time anyway but, because of the way we misplace incentives in public education, arrives there only at the very end of the school year with final exams. This is when kids ask, "So what do I really need to know?" And it is when teachers finally level with kids and say, "Okay, this is really what you need to know." This, too, should happen all year long, but generally does not. I'd been thinking about Peggy's comment that day I sat in Grace Haber's English class. She'd said how teachers should just give students the final exam questions

144

the first day they walk in the room. It makes a lot of sense really. We say we have clear objectives for what students are to learn, yet we always end up playing an end-of-the-year guessing game with kids about what's on the final. Next year, I decided, I would give students in my social studies classes a list of terms and a list of essay questions at the beginning of each unit and tell them the unit test will be made up from the two lists. They'd have the test items the first day they walk in the room. Instead of spending their energy anxiously guessing what's on the test, they'd spend their time studying what they know will be there.

But I was talking about June. Somebody, I can't remember who, has said that if aliens visited an American high school they would report that it is a place where the young go to watch adults work. Teachers spend all kinds of energy dreaming up supermotivational activities, pleading with students to get their work done, making sure they've covered all material that might possibly appear on the test, and then anxiously wait for the test results, worrying that some kids might not pass. Except for perhaps the minority of students, for whom admission to a select college is a matter of urgency, the consequences of academic mediocrity or even failure in high school are not great. One of the great strengths of the American education system is that it gives students a second chance—and a third and a fourth—with open enrollments to community colleges, state colleges with low admission standards and remediation programs, adult education facilities, special programs for high school dropouts, and more. All this, however, has the effect of minimizing the consequences of not taking high school academics seriously. As a result, many students don't. And for that reason, the adults sweat and worry, and so many students genially amble their way through the system.

As I was saying, in June you get a little bit of a feeling that it could be otherwise. Review sessions sprout up and students voluntarily attend. Teachers become less like deliverers of instruction and more like coaches and tutors to students who have suddenly found the right questions to ask. There's less concern about policing students who are not "on task," since the burden for learning has shifted to the students. I was giving an after-school review session one year in June, and when it was over a number of students said thank you. I was bowled over. Never before had students said thank you for giving them instruction. But now they were saying it because I had something that, for once, they desperately wanted: knowledge and, more important, an ability to convey it. And I was giving it to them cheerfully and skillfully. And they appreciated it. That should happen more often.

When exam time finally comes to Amesley (for ninth-graders and up), classes are suspended and both students and teachers show up only when they have an exam (or, in the case of teachers, a proctoring assignment). This is one of the more civilized features of life at Amesley High. Schools serve a custodial function in society as well as an educational function. For a brief week in June, we are relieved of our custodial responsibility and may focus solely on the real work at hand. Unlike most paper correcting during the school year, which I do in bits and pieces hastily between classes and late at night, the final exam essays get a careful read because for once I have time to read them.

June makes remarkably good sense educationally (except for seniors, who go belly up the instant they get their college acceptance letter), which is why, after exams are over and graded, there is one remaining school-year ritual (not graduation, although that is a ritual, too) that all teachers must endure before leaving for the summer. And it serves to remind us that we are after all but cogs in the great bureaucratic wheels of public education. Teachers across the country, I am sure, will attest to the universality of this ritual, though it takes on a particular style at Amesley. I refer to end-of-the-year signout. It's like a game, perhaps a scavenger hunt or an automobile road rally, only the goal is to extract your final paycheck from the claws of Bernice Fleischmann. Bernice Fleischmann?!

Yes. Years ago, Bernice refused to take on any clubs or sports so the principal at that time—long since gone, probably dead—assigned Bernice to head up end-of-the-year signout procedures, and she has been lord of the fiefdom ever since. There should be laws against it. There probably are.

Midway through exam week, Bernice distributes a checklist to all teachers, requiring the full signature (initials will not do, as I discovered one year) of the person in charge for each end-of-the-year item on the list. For example, item twenty-one is "Final exams neatly bundled in alphabetical order, tied with standard-grade twine, and placed in correct location in school vault." This is to be signed by June Henriksen of the main office. Heaven forbid that one not use standard-grade twine or have just one exam not alphabetically correct, or, as previously stated, not obtain a full signature. Bernice has been known to spot check. Some of the other items on the list are "All textbooks numbered and inventoried," "Classroom walls stripped bare (check for nail holes)," "All lesson plans filed chronologically in Dept. Chair's office," and "Homeroom cards with all absences accounted for."

This last one has been my downfall more than once. I generally give clerical tasks only peripheral attention and since most clerical tasks are by nature simple and routine, it suffices. But homeroom attendance cards are another story. I am certain that if just several volts of administrative brain power were applied to the matter of attendance procedures, the system could be greatly streamlined. But that has not happened yet, so we are left to struggle with the system as is. A half chevron in the upper right corner of the daily attendance box (of which there are 180 on each attendance card) signifies a morning absence. A half chevron in the lower left corner of a daily attendance box signifies an afternoon absence. A full chevron means absent all day. In case a student leaves and returns in the same day an asterisk is placed in the box. After each box has been thus marked, the correct letter drawn from the state-approved absence code must be written above the chevron or asterisk indicating the nature of the absence. An *S* means "ill." *X* means "illegal absence." *R* means "death in family." And so on. Additionally, each legal absence must be corroborated by a note signed by the parent or legal guardian, to be obtained from the student by the homeroom teacher.

Since this clerical task receives only the peripheral attention that I grant all other clerical tasks, I have big problems. Which are too embarrassing to go into here. Suffice it to say that I have been known to spend a full day after final exams are over rectifying my homeroom attendance cards in order to obtain the coveted full signature of June Henriksen so that I may extract my final paycheck from Bernice.

I wonder if Bernice would really withhold my paycheck if I failed to get all twenty-seven signatures.

Thus reminded, in our terminal act of the school year, of our lowly position in the great hierarchy of public education, we teachers dutifully obtain the needed signatures and with heads bowed low are granted our last paycheck for the next two and a half months.

And we go home for the summer.

I like to get away, at least for a few days, as soon as school is out. It's important to make a clean break and set a new pattern of routines for the summer. We used to go camping on such occasions. That was in the days when we could fit everything we needed in the trunk of our aging Japanese compact. Now that we are parents, things have changed. The one time we attempted camping, the car (now a wagon) was loaded to the ceiling, 90 percent of the stuff therein being the required life-support equipment for our normal four-month-old daughter. Lately, we find ourselves vacationing with Grammy and Grandpa as the child-care service is abundant and free. Or we rent a cabin on a lake and settle in for a week. This year we chose the latter and attempted to bring in everything we needed so that we wouldn't have to make any trips to the store. This proved to be nice in theory but in fact we found ourselves making daily sojourns to the nearest store, which was five miles away and had most things we needed in a quantity of one, at a price three times whatever civilization charges.

But we did manage to spend long spells just sitting by the lake reading or playing with Rebecca, watching how much sand she could stuff in her swimsuit. It was a good vacation; it was a change of pace and provided an opportunity to discard tired thoughts and fire up a few new synapses in the old brain.

It had been a rugged two years, what with the excitement of the PAE report and its ultimate descent to oblivion, the team thing debacle and Roberta's hasty departure, the principals' conference in New York and Bill Pierce's slow undoing. And now the experimental-school idea, which, if I'd learned anything from experience, would probably . . . well never mind, it's too depressing.

I find myself facing a dilemma. On the one hand, I wish to see change in the school where I work, so I labor in all manner of ways looking for a weak point in the system's walls where I may break through and reconfigure some small portion of the edifice. On the other hand, I grow increasingly persuaded that in order for real change to happen, the entire system of public education must be rethought, perhaps through the use of something like a choice scheme. So, while I am compelled to seek change in my little corner of the world where I have some influence and control, it is increasingly clear that what is called for is change at those lofty levels of policy making where my influence is virtually nil. I am left with a troubling question: given the present system, is attempting school reform at the local level an exercise in futility?

As I was beginning to say, while sitting by that lake I started to gain what only time and distance permit—perspective. All the trees were starting to come together and the overall shape of the forest was becoming clear. What had two years taught me? What worked? Given events as they played themselves out, it was easier to come up with a list of what didn't and probably won't work to make high schools better. So here's my list, direct from the shores of Lake Matokanac.

What Won't Work

1. *The Quick Fix.* Our system of public education has evolved, solidified, expired, calcified, and fossilized over a

period of many years. It is not subject to rapid change, given its present state. Possibly (probably?) it is not subject to any real change at all. To use another metaphor, maybe a more promising one, our system of public education is like a great, weighty fly wheel that has slowly gathered speed and force over more than a century. You can slow it down and maybe even stop it, but it will take time and tremendous pressure because of its awesome inertia.

2. *Making Small Adjustments to the System.* Mordecai Potter and his ilk will not bring about a revolution in education. Making small changes in classroom strategy (even ones that are not ludicrous) is not what is called for. The problem is not that the machine needs oil or fine tuning. It is that the machine is running to design standards that are no longer relevant.

3. *Coping Strategies.* Most of the consultants who travel the circuit preaching stress-reduction strategies, effective discipline techniques, humor in the classroom, et cetera are like charlatan doctors selling syrupy panaceas to gravely ill patients. They anesthetize us to the pain rather than routing the cancer.

4. *The Present Structure of Incentives.* As things presently are, teachers worry more about the academic success of their students than students themselves. That is because the immediate consequences of academic failure, in general, fall more heavily on the teacher than they do on the student. As I've pointed out, this country is great at providing second chances (and third and fourth and fifth), which in itself is great and compassionate, but one very unfortunate result is the erosion of effort in high school. The high school diploma has become little more than a certificate of attendance.

5. *The Belief That Education Reform Will Solve All Our Problems.* Let's suppose we decentralize the system as I've suggested, and we greatly reduce the number of students that teachers work with, and we also restructure the school day to allow for an interdisciplinary approach, and we redesign teacher education, and we bring on board the best and the brightest eager young teachers we can find, and we pay them

what physicians in this country get. I predict we will see a significant but still only modest improvement in educational outcomes. The fact remains that school, no matter how good, is just one part of a kid's growing-up experience. The more powerful factors are the home and the culture in general. We will probably never achieve the kinds of high learning outcomes that we envy in Japan and Germany and France because our culture does not support education the way those cultures do. Good schools will not solve all our problems. But they are an important part of an overall prescription for societal well-being.

That's my list. As I said, it's easier to figure out what hasn't worked than to prescribe what will. But having completed the former, and as the mosquitoes were strangely absent, I continued to ponder what might work.

What Might Work

The United States has experienced wave after wave of so-called school reform during the last hundred years, yet the shape of American public education remains essentially unchanged. Why? More important, given the overwhelming consensus that schools *must* change, how may reformers prevail this time around?

There is no lack of imaginative ideas for school reorganization. Indeed, many "new" ideas we read about are only updated versions from past reform eras. The problem is, as it always has been, putting imaginative ideas into practice and getting them to stick.

Education's resistance to change is rooted in the system itself. The system is vast, uncoordinated, hugely bureaucratic, and monopolistic. Varied interests including unions, school administrators, school board members, state education departments, university schools of education, citizen groups, politicians, and political appointees all vie for control of the system but none has enough power to force its own agenda.

Do not be deceived! This is not a carefully crafted system of power sharing with rational checks and balances. It is what it is: a mess. Imagine a corporation made up entirely of minority shareholders each with a slightly different view of how things ought to be. Now imagine that this corporation enjoys a monopoly and furthermore that the state guarantees the corporation's solvency come what may. That's public education. A cynical view? Just look at the record of school reform in this country.

It seems then that nothing short of a complete dismantling of the system will bring about real change. Indeed. So why not? Why not dismantle the system? Here's how: make available to parents one voucher for each school-age child equal in value to the local school district's per-pupil expenditure, redeemable at any accredited school. That's it. A simple and revolutionary idea, one which I used to regard with as much hostility as do most people in public education. But after my experiences of the last two years, I've begun to think it may be the only way to go. If we take it, our problems will not be solved overnight (despite the enthusiasm of their most avid supporters, vouchers are not a quick fix), but the underlying incentives could be realigned in a more promising way so that over the course of time, a better system of schooling might emerge.

Here are the possible advantages:

1. For the first time, there will be *real* opportunities for entrepreneurship and innovation in public education. Like-minded school people with an idea will be able to set up a school of their own and open for business. If their idea is good, it will have a real chance to catch on. If it's not good or if it is not well presented, the school will fold. Is that so bad? As it is, innovators are forced into the private sector where their clientele are the wealthy few who can afford unsubsidized private education. Under a voucher system, these same innovators could set up a school in the inner city and still have available a ready revenue source. Everybody, rich and poor alike, gets the vouchers.

2. Competition will be unleashed on the profession of education. As it is, bad public schools are not *really* threatened with closure. (When is the last time state officials closed

a public school for poor performance?) And good schools receive no substantial reward. A little competition would remedy that quickly. In addition, I predict that a variety of schools with differing philosophies, alternative methods, and new forms of organization would emerge. A hundred flowers would blossom.

3. Parents would get to choose their children's school. Currently, we get to choose our doctors, lawyers, and legislators. Why not our schools, too?

I'll anticipate some questions.

1. *What will happen to existing public schools?* "Public school" will be redefined. Any school that subjects itself to a state accreditation process will be public. That will include existing public schools as well as a lot of schools at present considered private. As for the buildings that presently house public schools, if the schools are good, they will continue to be used as they are. If parents pull their children out and numbers decline, I would recommend the authorities lease space to one or more of the "private" (in this case equally public) schools where the children are being sent.

2. *Won't vouchers lead to segregation?* It would be hard to create a system more segregated than the present one. Look around. Wealthy suburban districts are almost exclusively white and affluent. If a voucher system were intelligently structured, there could be built-in incentives for schools to achieve an ethnic and socioeconomic balance. Such incentives exist in higher education, where grant money is sometimes tied to pledges of affirmative action in student admissions and faculty hiring. Nothing helps people see the light of reason and tolerance so well as fiscal necessity.

3. *Since some school districts spend more money per student than others, won't the value of vouchers vary?* The present system of school taxation is part of the problem.[1] Since school revenues are tied to property taxes and property taxes vary widely from community to community, the amount of money that gets spent per student varies widely as well. It is not uncommon for a suburban district to spend two or even three times per student what its city counterpart spends. That is a

fundamental inequity of the system. And moving to a voucher program provides the opportunity to address it. First, make state government the collecting authority for school taxes. When all the tax money comes in, the state then carves up the pie so that all school-age children receive an equal share in the form of vouchers whose value is equalized (with some adjustments for regional differences in cost of living).

4. *Won't residents of wealthy communities feel cheated?* Yes, residents of wealthy communities *will* feel cheated and will no doubt put up a fight to save the privileged education they feel their children deserve just because the parents can afford it. The ensuing struggle will be a classic face-off between the power of privilege and the principle of equality of opportunity. It is a battle that will not be easily won.

5. *What about schools espousing a religious point of view? Would they be eligible to receive vouchers?* Society presently supports religious institutions. Huge tax concessions are granted to churches and church-affiliated schools. Public school districts are presently required to provide certain services to private (religious) schools within their jurisdiction, and private colleges with church affiliation receive regular subsidy by way of grants and state-supported scholarships. While the Bill of Rights forbids state-established religion, it also prohibits the state from restricting the free exercise thereof. It has always been a balancing act and will be no more than that under a voucher system.

6. *Won't a voucher system exploit poor people?* On the contrary, a voucher system will give poor people real options for a change. Their children will not automatically be consigned to a drug-infested school with inadequate resources. To those critics who say poor people are not savvy enough to choose a good school, I say that is paternalistic garbage. Since we entrust all citizens rich and poor with the responsibility to vote, may we reasonably deny certain people the responsibility to choose their children's school just because some of us think some others of us aren't informed enough? Vouchers will empower poor people and the rich are always afraid of empowering the poor.

7. *As a teacher, shouldn't I be concerned that vouchers will erode the hard-won gains that teacher unions have made over the years?* As Jerry Rubicon said, unions organized to build collective power among workers who individually had little. If we move to a voucher system, individual teachers gain greater power. They can hang out their shingle and open for business in the same way a physician or an attorney opens a private practice. They become players in a competitive system and succeed or fail on their own abilities.

8. *Will vouchers solve all our education ills?* Of course not. Some ills will be cured, new ones will appear. But tallying up the relative benefits and problems of each system, I conclude that a voucher system deserves at least our serious consideration.

But vouchers are not the whole answer. They provide a starting point. They create the opportunity for innovation to occur. What we then need are sensible ideas put into practice. I know how I'd set up my high school. How about this for starters: base high school graduation on mastery. In other words, chuck the requirements for attendance, credits, hours of instruction, and standardized tests, and in their place fashion a list of performance-based goals that a student must achieve in order to be granted a diploma. Then let those goals drive the whole program.

Well, I hear the critics grumbling, that sounds very nice, but who is to judge what "intelligently" means? What is the standard? Where is the cut-off point?

Here are my answers. First, the faculty of the school judges the standard. Imagine a committee of teachers who hear a student present his or her oral commentary. They then render their collective judgment. Second, as for the standard, we will know schools by their graduates. In time schools will gain reputations for high standards or low standards, and there will be pressure on those with low standards to raise them—real pressure since, when the word gets out, parents will stop sending their kids there. Look at higher education in this country. It's easy to tell which colleges have high standards, and it's not because of standardized tests, it's because of the college's reputation, something a little more elusive but much more meaningful.

The beauty of a voucher system is that people get to disagree and still get their way. Not everybody has to buy my idea about goals driving the program. Those who don't, send their kids to somebody else's school. They do what they want. I do what I want. Over time perhaps we will see who was right. Or maybe we will see that we were both right; that for different kids, different kinds of schools are needed. Which leads me to my next point.

We assume in this country that all kids are the same. Of course, no educated adult would ever *say* that, but the assumption is clearly there. It is embedded in our school system. Virtually all our public schools, particularly our high schools, are essentially alike: bells, periods, subjects, lectures, credits, multiple-guess tests. We rarely come right out and say it, but the system speaks for us. We force all kids through the same mold. If there is one thing on which both research and common sense agree, it is that kids are not the same, that they learn in different ways, that they respond to different kinds of incentives. Therefore, it is painfully obvious (painful because we take no action despite the obviousness) that we need to create alternatives.

Different schools for different kids.

This is where the critics say, watch out, Nehring, you are creating an opening for racial and sectarian divisiveness that our public schools have spent a century trying to eradicate. I don't think we need to fear. Look again at higher education. The United States has all kinds of colleges and universities. There are big state institutions and small, intimate, private colleges. There are Jewish schools and Catholic schools. There are technical institutes and schools for the arts. There are traditional colleges and colleges with experimental curricula. Has all of this led to divisiveness? I see no evidence of it. Divisiveness, no. Diversity, yes. And that's good.

Assuming that I now have my school where goals drive the program. I would suggest that we next tackle the problem of numbers. There is no good reason why teachers should have to meet with 120 kids a day, as they typically do. As we've already seen, if you tally up all the professional educators (teachers, counselors, administrators) in a typical high school and all the students and reduce it to a ratio, you get something like one to thirteen. Those are very attractive numbers. To achieve them, we educators have simply (and profoundly) to change our attitudes. We must stop viewing ourselves as subject-area specialists and begin to see ourselves as generalists. Accepting that, we will then be able to design learning experiences that involve interaction with far fewer kids.

A final suggestion. Let's get away from the idea, increasingly practiced, that people called "curriculum specialists" should develop courses that then get "implemented" by teachers. It assumes that teaching is a very neat technical procedure, and dictates accordingly that "experts" design the procedure and leave it to the technicians (teachers) to carry it out as a simple matter of following directions. Inconveniently for our technocratic world, good teaching has never worked that way. That is because good teaching is a quirky blend of personality, scholarship, style, intuition, training, planning, luck, and constant readjustment. It is the product of good chemistry between a particular teacher and a particular group of students. Most good teachers pay little heed to the voluminous curriculum guides they are handed. They know better. We'll be much better off if we fire all the curriculum specialists and give practitioners more time to reflect upon and plan for their own work with their own students.

8.

What I Did
on My Summer Vacation

I did not spend my entire week at Lake Matokanac making notes on education. I promise. Truth be told, most of it was spent drinking too much overpriced cheap beer (from the aforementioned purveyor) and eating too much heavily greased, salted, and sugared food with alarmingly low nutritional value. Thus, we returned home to Amesley at the end of the week tanned, relaxed, and vowing temperance for at least the next six months.

Every summer I work at the state education department. The week following Lake Matokanac was to be my annual State Ed week, which gave my temperance vow its first serious challenge. They call me a consultant, but that is a glorified title. What I do is read student essays collected from all over the state and brought to that great nerve center of pedagogy where they are collated, read, classified, scrutinized, and generally turned into grist for the statewide test mill by establishing things like validity and reliability and accountability and cover-your-assability (pardon my French) for the bureaus that construct them, which are wont to be sued by parents aggravated by the fact that their child did not graduate because he or she did not pass THAT TEST. So I come in for a week and I and five other "consultants" evaluate about a thousand essays each. No, I'm *not* sure why I do it. So I won't attempt to say. What I'll say is what I learn about State Ed while I'm there. (Maybe that's why I do it.)

State Ed is where policy is made. People work at a relaxed pace there. You can go and get coffee and snacks at the cafeteria whenever you like. The halls are quiet and orderly. The atmosphere is hushed. People are friendly and smile a lot. Workers generally arrive at 8:00 or 9:00 and leave between 3:00 and 5:00. They seem relaxed on the commuter bus. They read novels. No matter where you work, there's a bathroom nearby. There's plenty of office equipment: phones, copy machines, fax machines, computers. There are plenty of support people: secretaries, custodians, security guards. Basically, it is very unlike your typical school. And as I said, this is where education policy is made. These are the people who make it. In a way, working at State Ed is kind of what teaching would be like if you took away the kids: you write lesson plans and tests, grade papers, and confer with colleagues.

In New York, education is governed by a group of amateurs. Truly. A cross section of the citizenry—the doctor, the lawyer, the plumber, the homemaker—collectively called the Board of Regents. The commissioner of education, whom they hire, brings matters of policy before them and they vote.

I imagine them in the control room of a great ship. A bank of levers stands before them. Being amateurs, they are not entirely sure what the levers do. But they have been left in charge so they need to find out. Of course, being well intending, they don't want to do anything drastic. What they don't understand is that moving one of those levers even a little bit has huge consequences. So they say, okay, let's see what happens if we move this one right here a little. And they put their hands on the lever, give it what seems like a gentle tug, and the whole ship rocks to the left (sparks fly, people fall out of chairs à la Star Trek). So then they say, oh no no no oh my goodness, and they race to the other end of the bank of levers, and in hope of compensating give one of those other levers a panicky tug, which of course results in the same flying sparks and people-falling-out-of-chairs scene only in reverse. This goes on until they begin to figure out how to restore calm to the control room. This may be achieved by firing the commissioner. Sometimes, one of the regents begins to understand what the levers do, but then his or term is up, and since terms rotate, you never really have anybody up there in the control room who knows what's going on and can do something about it. Of course, the commissioner is very aware of what happens when you pull those levers but he is not eager to tell the bosses they're wrong. The commissioner, however, at least gets to brace himself before the ship starts rocking, something those of us who are not in the control room do not get to do.

During my week at State Ed, I thought some more about goals. I guess that's what people at State Ed in the absence of kids are *supposed* to think about. And furthermore, it occurred to me that everything I'd been yapping about and fighting for during these last two years would suggest that when attempting to establish an experimental high school program, the place to begin would be with a summary list ("no longer than a page" as I'd said in my newspaper article) of educational goals for our students, and then design a program to fit those goals.

The more I thought about it, the more daunted I felt by the prospect of sitting down with a group of colleagues and trying to agree on a list of, say, ten things that make up a high school education. Furthermore, even if we came up with such a list, it would have very little credibility for the public since the public would have had no role in creating this list of goals in the first place. So then I thought, well maybe a committee of professionals and laypersons could be established to put together this list. And then I realized, no, that wouldn't work because we'd spend the next three years disagreeing on what our goals should be and we'd never get around to setting up a program, which was, after all, our overarching goal. Then I had an idea.

Maybe somewhere within the hallowed halls of State

Ed sitting on a shelf in some dusty office is such a list of goals for education in our great state that at some time in the past was hammered out by some blue-ribbon committee to put out some political brush fire of the moment and having served its purpose now lies forgotten in a stack of other reports in some small office somewhere. The more I thought about it, the more convinced I became that such a thing must exist, that somebody must have asked this very question at some time in the past and that the trick would be to locate which hallowed hall and which dusty office and which stack of reports within this great maze of offices and bureaus and departments and divisions within this great nerve center of pedagogy that we call State Ed.

So I wrote a letter to the good commissioner. "We are trying to set up an experimental school . . . could you furnish me with a summary list of goals . . . thank you very much . . ." Two weeks later a UPS package arrived at my door. The return address read "State Education Department" but no office was indicated. Inside was a very thick document, about two hundred pages deep, with no cover letter. The document announced itself as "Evaluation of the Regents Action Plan of New York State Fourth Annual Report." It was full of charts and graphs and impressive-sounding text and footnotes and appendices. I imagined it must have resulted from some previous occasion when a lever was moved and the sparks flew and people fell out of chairs and teams of damage-control specialists scurried across all decks and the ship rocked heavily and this report emerged. So I wrote the good commissioner again. "I think I received your reply but I'm not sure. If it is your reply, it's not what I asked for . . . maybe I didn't make myself clear . . . what I really need is . . . thank you very much . . ."

While waiting for an answer to my second letter, I decided to take further action myself. While in the great capital city one afternoon on unrelated business, I stopped by the State Ed office of my neighbor Edna Cosgrove. I explained my situation. No problem, Edna said. If my sought-after list existed anywhere it would most likely be in one of four offices. She then produced an organizational chart for State Ed. It was a book really, since whoever had designed it apparently abandoned the idea of fitting everything on one sheet. It was about fifty pages long and required special skill to be navigated. Edna gave me the pages for the four offices. I thanked her and was on my way.

Now here comes the incredible part. The first office I entered belonged to somebody with a title like assistant deputy to the deputy assistant commissioner in charge of quality assurance and oversight evaluation control. Whatever. I was greeted by a pleasant lady behind a desk. I told her what I wanted. "Oh yes," she said. "We have that right over here." She went to a file cabinet across the office, pulled out a document, and handed it to me. It was exactly what I was looking for. A summary list of ten learning goals for kids in New York State. What every graduate should know to get a high school diploma.

Two weeks later I received a second large envelope from State Ed. This time with a very nice letter from an associate within the Bureau of X within the department of Y within the division of Z who told me that such a summary list does not exist and that the enclosed "booklet" (about two hundred pages thick) was all they had.

At any rate our experimental-school planning group (yet to be formed) would now have a starting point: ten simple goals that would drive our work.

The absurdity of this whole tale reminds me of a comment that a student made in one of those one thousand essays I read during my week of temperance. He wrote, "The twentieth century sounds exciting to me but it's gonna ruin us when it comes."

State Ed is firmly into the twentieth century, a century that has been all about bureaucracy and legalization, which leads me to a point that I must make before finishing this book.

Public schools are becoming increasingly legalistic institutions. State and federal law, commissioner of education regulations (which have the force of law), and court decisions play an ever-expanding role in the governance of individual schools. Laws and regulations specify the number of days of instruction, course content, building architecture, hiring and firing practices, remediation practices, school lunch prices, school bus design, professional roles, professional certification, treatment of the handicapped, definition of handicapping conditions, and more. As a student makes her way from kindergarten (which may soon be mandated to last the full day) to high school graduation (for which commissioner's regulations specify so many Carnegie units of credit), her experience is guided by the unseen hands of legislators, judges, and high-ranking bureaucrats. And from the time she enters kindergarten to the time she graduates, the sheer volume of law guiding her way will no doubt increase almost exponentially.

To the extent that laws, court decisions, and regulations proliferate, the decision-making power of local school officials and teachers is diminished. This is the process of legalization—the replacement of judgment with policy, the elimination of the requirement that local officials scrutinize, evaluate, and take action upon a particular human situation, replaced with increasing reliance on procedures and established policy, defined at higher levels.

Is legalization in schools good or bad? The extent to which schools are desegregated in this country is largely the result of legal initiatives. That's good. Increased access to schools for physically handicapped students is largely the result of laws. That, too, is good. Improved salaries for chronically underpaid teachers in recent years are in many states the result of action by the state legislature. That's good, too. On the other hand, many school people—teachers and administrators—complain that their ability to educate kids is seriously impaired by the laws and regulations they must adhere to.

Clearly, a balance between law and local discretion is needed. The question is whether that balance has been thrown off by the weighty body of existing law. If it has, then those laws, though well-intended, are counterproductive. Is this indeed the case? On the whole, I think so. Here's an illustration. Though by no means a comprehensive argument against the proliferation of school law, it is intended to illuminate one small field of the educational landscape.

In 1984, the New York State Board of Regents adopted a statement of goals for K–12 education.[1] This statement outlines ten criteria for high school graduation, ten things kids need to know or be able to do in order to get a high school diploma in New York State. In a world of increasingly complex laws and regulations, this statement stands out. It is elegant in its simplicity, powerful because of its directness and clarity. It is, I daresay, almost a wonder to behold.

According to the statement, it is intended as the guiding force for education policy in the state. From it, and for its ends, one must assume, come all the laws and regulations that govern public education, the greatest commandment on which are based all the scriptures.

And so it is. In direct relation to these goals stand numerous course syllabi in numerous subject areas, the overarching goal of which is to serve this statement. To see that these syllabi are adhered to, clearly defined certification criteria have been established for the instructors who will implement the syllabi. Furthermore, to see that the objectives of the syllabi have been met, there are tests developed centrally at the state education department and standardized to ensure that all students everywhere are held to the same standard. In addition, to ensure that all the course syllabi, in the correct proportion, are administered, units of course credit have been assigned and programs of study specifying the distribution of course credit, again, so that all students everywhere will learn the subjects in their proper balance. Finally, to ensure that all students are guaranteed adequate time to master the course syllabi, the number of hours of instruction are also clearly specified for each unit of credit. Thus, the wheels of the state education bureaucracy, though slow, turn in response to the Regents' goals and facilitate learning across the state, the model of a well-functioning bureaucracy, efficiently serving the needs of a democracy.

Or so it appears. In practice, the effect of all this highly rational behavior turns out to be anything but. In practice, it becomes clear that all the highly rational behavior causes simply, as Arthur Wise has suggested in a book about legalization in education, "more bureaucratic overlay without attaining the intended policy objectives."[2] It is, as Wise calls it, hyperrationalization.

How does this occur? Very simply, the learning goals become overwhelmed by the bureaucratic machinery. The policies and regulations established to achieve the goals become an end in themselves. Rarely does anyone within the bureaucracy (or above or below it) ask whether a student has actually achieved the original goals. Instead we ask, has the student received the correct number of hours of instruction? Has the student been instructed by a certified teacher? Has the syllabus been adhered to? Has the student scored above a minimum reference point on a standardized test? Has the student accumulated the correct number of course credits? In the correct proportion? At no time does the system demand that the student demonstrate that she can do what the Regents' goal says she must be able to do.

In practice, then, the system specifies certain bureaucratic norms and sees to it that they are adhered to on the assumption that this will ensure that the Regents' goals have been met. This assumption is erroneous. As any schoolteacher will tell you, many of our high school graduates can't do diddly.

The only way to ensure that the Regents' goals have been met is to demand that each student clearly demonstrate mastery of each goal by way of a meaningful examination.

What do I mean? Here is an examination that would test mastery of several of the Regents' goals: given three stories from the front page of a major newspaper, the student must be able to comment intelligently in writing and before a faculty committee on any two. It's that simple.

And that unlikely. A bureaucratically driven system cannot process "intelligent commentary." Although a community of scholars (such as school faculty) *can*, the system is driven not by their judgment (legalization has circumvented locally based judgment, remember), but by bureaucratic norms. Measurable criteria only, please.

What are the prospects for the future? Unless enlightened leaders are put in place, I fear the legalization train will continue to pick up speed and freight. It will take a very conscious and politically courageous effort by leaders at all levels to bring it under control.

*   *   *

Most summers, against my better judgment, I end up taking a course at the state university nearby, usually in the college of education. Like other cogs (unions, school boards, state education departments) that make up the slow-turning wheels of the great machine of public education in this country, colleges of education have their pluses and minuses. The great plus of a college of education from the standpoint of a practitioner is that it can serve as a ready resource, a huge data base, for a whole range of educational issues. The great minus is that most of the professors possess a great deal of knowledge, very little of which is based on experience in a public school classroom. Like peacocks spreading their feathers, they look big and impressive, but behind the huge display there's often very little credible substance. Consequently, in most of the education courses I've undertaken, there's a strong undercurrent of tension between teacher (one year's experience as classroom teacher, then left, disgusted, to return to graduate school; earned doctorate, twenty years as professor, edits series on curriculum studies) and the students (classroom teachers with an average of ten years' experience in public schools, but not well versed in research findings). Each side suspects the other's base of experience.

But we've already said all that.

Apart from learning whatever I'm supposed to learn in the course I'm taking any given summer, I also learn a great deal of empathy for my own students, and I gain insight into classroom dynamics by occupying a student desk for a change instead of standing at the chalkboard. For instance, I learned from the course I took one summer (Principles of School Management) that behavior among graduate students, ranging in age from their early twenties to their fifties, has a great deal in common with that of my own ninth- and tenth-graders. We were faced with a major research paper as a requirement for the course. The teacher said it had to be fifteen pages minimum, and sure enough from the front row a man who must have been in his fifties asked if that meant single spaced or double spaced. Then a woman who I know has taught for at least ten years asked if a page meant front side of a sheet only or front and back. In this course we also took a midterm exam. When we got the exam back during the next class, one mature-looking woman in the front row, on seeing a low grade circled at the top of her paper, threw the test to the floor, harumphed loudly, and pouted, arms crossed, for the rest of the class. And of course, before the final exam everybody asked what's gonna be on the test, to which the professor smugly replied, "Everything."

In this class, I also learned something of what was taught, that is, why school management is so messed up. Actually that was not the intent of the course. The intent of the course was to teach me how to manage a school. But most of that boiled down to theories of manipulation, how a school principal can control information or create a psychological climate conducive to getting his or her way. For instance, there are great strategies for participatory management, which create the charade that teachers are indeed participating in important school policy decisions. But ultimately, the principal or the superintendent still makes the decision. And how could it be any other way? The teachers are tenured. They can be removed only for gross and heinous acts. Most principals, however, never stay around long enough to get tenure and most superintendents are not in tenurable positions. Therefore, they work at the pleasure of the board. When decisions are made, they're under the gun. It's their jobs on the line, not the teachers'. The whole concept of shared decision making or participatory management is and will remain vacuous until the roles and the burden of accountability of the players change.

Epilogue

All good things must end, and so does summer vacation. Back-to-school ads come earlier every year. It used to be that advertisers would wait until about August 15, which was bad enough, but it now seems the first back-to-school ads start to appear around the third week in July. The first one of the season always sends a shiver up my back. I mentally protest that I'm not supposed to be thinking about school yet and it's unfair for advertisers to create the illusion of imminence when in fact school is still maybe six or seven weeks away.

Usually, there is enough turmoil in my soul (engendered by repeated pictures of happy children carrying new lunch boxes and wearing the latest fashions) that by the first or second week in August I force myself into school for a good several days to plan out the first unit for each of the courses I'll be teaching. For those few days, I labor mightily, preparing new lesson plans, reading new material, reorganizing my courses, and trying to leave the room truly prepared so that all I have left to do is walk in on day one and start teaching. Of course, there are always glitches. The schedule I was given in June has changed and I'll be teaching the "slow" group of tenth-graders instead of the "honors" group. Or the copy machine is broken (again) and the repair person isn't scheduled to come for another week. Or there's a shortage of textbooks so that for the first three weeks or so until more come in, half of my students will not have their own book. The list goes on. But at least I'm about 90 percent ready to go most of the time when I leave the school building after my week of voluntary curriculum development.

And I live in a kind of euphoria for the last couple weeks of summer, secure in the knowledge that I'm basically ready. The anxiety dreams about not being prepared and students misbehaving, which I experience regularly after the appearance of the first back-to-school ad, are replaced by totally non-school-related dreams. About this time, the August sky seems to turn a deeper blue. The air is drier and cooler. The night sky has more stars. And I find myself *noticing* the night sky more often, sitting in the back yard and taking in the late summer evenings. I start to feel nostalgic about the opening of school. Despite all the problems, I want to go back.

The first day back is always meetings. And more meetings. We didn't get to see our new principal because they hadn't hired one yet. The principal search committee had selected their top candidate and then learned the top candidate was backing out. So they reopened the search and O. J. Dave assured us in his back-to-school pep talk that we would have a principal by the end of the week. Meantime, George Handelman would be at the helm.

I ran into Bill Pierce in the men's room between meetings. He seemed refreshed by the summer. He didn't look as tired. And he said he felt good about coming back. He was ready to teach, he said. I was glad to hear that from my friend.

I was washing my hands at the sink and Bill stepped over to a stall nearby. When he opened the door he exclaimed suddenly, "Oh my god!"

I stopped washing my hands and stood there with the water dripping off my fingers, not exactly sure what I should do or say.

"Ah . . . what . . . ah . . . Is everything okay there, pardner?"

"Oh yeah, fine." Bill replied resuming a normal, non-alarmed voice. "It's just kind of ironic. That's all."

"What's that?" I asked.

"Come 'ere," said Bill, motioning me over toward the stall. "Look," said Bill. "Up against the wall there."

I looked. There, screwed up against the wall of the stall, was a shiny new chrome toilet paper dispenser, and in its metal arms, held gently aloft, was a *roll* of paper.

Change *had* come to Amesley High School after all. The faculty petition had worked. Two years later, this was Roberta's answer. Whatever Roberta's intent, her little joke (was it a challenge or a taunt?) restored my sense of humor. And I began to feel that maybe, just maybe, we could get this little experimental school up and running.

Through all the meetings, there was little official talk of plans for our program. Good. The first day back is never a good time to begin serious discussion about a new project. People are just trying to get their bearings. In a week or two, I figured, we could get to work on it. This project had been two years coming and I'd learned to be patient. If real change was going to come to Amesley, it could not be forced. (Pushed, maybe.)

I'd also learned not to hold my breath waiting for bold new departures. And I'd learned not to be crushed when things don't turn out. I'd learned, maybe unfortunately, not to invest my soul in attempting school reform, but to work doggedly and do my best at it nonetheless. I've wondered at times which is the better metaphor for such efforts at change. Is it the little engine that could, which, undaunted by the height of the mountain and the weight of the very full train, starts up and through sheer will power makes it? Or is it Sisyphus, rolling the stone up the hill only to have it tumble back down as he nears the top, then trying again and again in futility?

If change comes to public education, it will be because people are persuaded the schools we have need serious fixing and are moved to fix them. If significant change does not come, it will be because—and this is a chilling thought—people believe that what we already have is good enough.

Notes

Chapter 1

1. For an up-to-date picture of urban public education, see Jonathan Kozol, *Savage Inequalities* (New York: Crown, 1991). Kozol shines a very intense spotlight on some of the very darkest corners of American public education. His descriptions sound like places in the Third World, but they are disturbingly close by (East St. Louis, Chicago), all just down the road from Amesley.

2. A. G. Powell, E. Farrar, and D. K. Cohen, *The Shopping Mall High School* (Boston: Houghton Mifflin, 1984). This is one of three books that resulted from a project cosponsored by the National Association of Secondary School Principals and the National Association of Independent Schools. The other two are Theodore Sizer's *Horace's Compromise* and Robert Hampel's *The Last Little Citadel* (see below). Together, they represent an excellent study of the contemporary high school.

3.   Theodore R. Sizer, *Horace's Compromise* (Boston: Hough-
     ton Mifflin, 1984).
4.   Ernest L. Boyer, *High School* (New York: HarperCollins,
     1983), p. 57. Boyer's empirically based study of high
     school is valuable both for the authority that such a large
     study necessarily commands and for the considerable
     insight the author brings to bear on the data.
5.   For the history of American public education, together
     the following titles draw a fairly comprehensive picture.
     Bowles and Gintis, in particular, give a much-needed
     critical analysis of public education's role in the context
     of a capitalist society. Bowles, Samuel, and Herbert Gin-
     tis. *Schooling in Capitalist America: Educational Reform
     and the Contradiction of Economic Life.* New York: Basic
     Books, 1976; Cremin, Lawrence Arthur. *American Educa-
     tion, the National Experience.* New York: HarperCollins,
     1980; Cremin, Lawrence Arthur. *American Education, the
     Metropolitan Experience, 1876–1980.* New York: Harper-
     Collins, 1988; Hampel, Robert L. *The Last Little Citadel:
     American High Schools Since 1940.* Boston: Houghton Mif-
     flin, 1986; Ravitch, Diane. *The Troubled Crusade: Ameri-
     can Education, 1945–1980.* New York: Basic Books, 1983.
6.   Report of the National Commission on Excellence in Edu-
     cation, *A Nation at Risk: The Imperative for Educational
     Reform: A Report to the Nation and the Secretary of Edu-
     cation* (Washington: United States Department of Educa-
     tion, Government Printing Office, 1983).

Chapter 2

1.   John I. Goodlad, *Teachers for Our Nation's Schools* (San
     Francisco: Jossey-Bass, 1990).
2.   *The 1991 Information Please Almanac* (Boston: Houghton
     Mifflin, 1990), p. 145.
3.   Terry Moe and John Chubb, *Politics, Markets, and America's
     Schools* (Washington, D.C.: Brookings Institute, 1990).
4.   Myron Lieberman, *Privatization and Educational Choice*
     (New York: St. Martin's Press, 1989).

Chapter 4

1. See Mark Starr, "Not a Miracle Cure," in *Newsweek,* Sept. 17, 1990, p. 60. Also, "Chelsea Schools Gain a Big Brother," *U.S. News & World Report,* Dec. 12, 1988, p. 13.
2. John L. Goodlad, *Teachers for Our Nation's Schools* (San Francisco: Jossey-Bass, 1990). See especially Chapter 5, "Teachers of Teachers," p. 154ff.
3. On Learning Styles, see Anthony F. Gregorc and Kathleen A. Butler, "Learning Is a Matter of Style," in *Vocational Education,* vol. 59, no. 3, pp. 27–29, April 1984. For a review of cooperative learning techniques, see Ron Brandt, "On Cooperation in Schools: A Conversation with David and Roger Johnson," in *Educational Leadership,* vol. 45, no. 3, pp. 14–19, Nov. 1987; and Robert E. Slavin, "Cooperative Learning and the Cooperative School," in *Educational Leadership,* vol. 45, no. 3, pp. 7–13, Nov. 1987. For a summary and critique of Hunter's program as well as a critique of educational faddism generally, see Robert E. Slavin, "PET and the Pendulum: Faddism in Education and How to Stop It," in *Phi Delta Kappan,* June 1989. For a review and critique of authentic assessment, see Gene Maeroff, "Assessing Alternative Assessment," in *Phi Delta Kappan,* December 1991.
4. The schools described here are fictional. They represent types of exceptional schools that are scattered all too sparingly across the education landscape.
5. Moe and Chubb, *Politics, Markets, and America's Schools.*

Chapter 7

1. See Jonathan Kozol, *Savage Inequalities.* Kozol's book is a long-overdue exposé of the truly savage inequalities of funding between suburban and inner-city schools. Kozol rejects voucher schemes and has serious reservations about choice. The choice scheme he writes most about, however, is the magnet-school concept, which is just one way of giving parents greater decision-making power.

There are other, more promising versions, such as that in place in District 4 in East Harlem (to which Kozol makes only passing reference), and in Cambridge, Massachusetts.

Chapter 8

1. "Statement of Regents Goals for Elementary and Secondary School Students," in *Proposed Regents School Improvement and Accountability Program for Public Schools,* "Appendix A," the University of the State of New York, the State Education Department, 1989. As this book goes to press, New York State is putting into place an initiative called "The New Compact for Learning," which promises to eliminate much red tape and grant local schools much greater autonomy. Time will tell how well it succeeds.
2. Arthur E. Wise. *Legislated Learning: The Bureaucratization of the American Classroom* (Berkeley and Los Angeles: University of California Press, 1979).